studysync®

Reading & Writing Companion

The Power of One

How do we stand out from the crowd?

studysync

studysync.com

Copyright © BookheadEd Learning, LLC
All Rights Reserved.

Send all inquiries to:
BookheadEd Learning, LLC
610 Daniel Young Drive
Sonoma, CA 95476

ISBN 978-1-94-469584-2

12 13 14 15 QSX 24 23 22
C

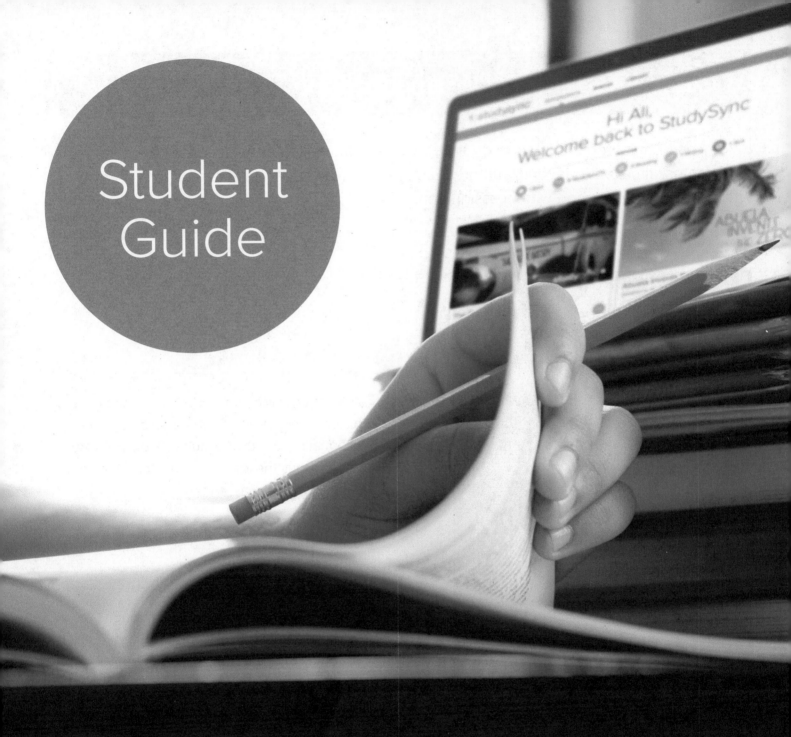

Student Guide

Getting Started

Welcome to the StudySync Reading & Writing Companion! In this book, you will find a collection of readings based on the theme of the unit you are studying. As you work through the readings, you will be asked to answer questions and perform a variety of tasks designed to help you closely analyze and understand each text selection. Read on for an explanation of each

Close Reading and Writing Routine

In each unit, you will read texts that share a common theme, despite their different genres, time periods, and authors. Each reading encourages a closer look through questions and a short writing assignment.

Rikki-Tikki-Tavi
FICTION
Rudyard Kipling
1894

1 Introduction   **study**sync●

" **R**ikki-Tikki-Tavi" is one of the most famous tales from *The Jungle Book*, a collection of short stories published in 1894 by English author Rudyard Kipling (1865–1936). The stories in *The Jungle Book* feature animal characters with anthropomorphic traits and are intended to be read as fables, each illustrating a moral lesson. In this story, Rikki-tikki-tavi is a courageous young mongoose adopted as a pet by a British family living in 19th-century colonial India.

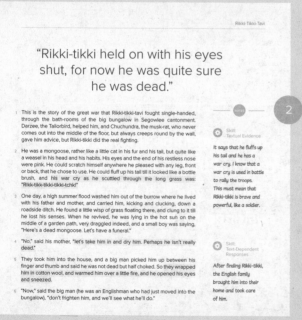

Rikki-Tikki-Tavi

"Rikki-tikki held on with his eyes shut, for now he was quite sure he was dead."

1 This is the story of the great war that Rikki-tikki-tavi fought single-handed, through the bath-rooms of the big bungalow in Segowlee cantonment. Darzee, the Tailorbird, helped him, and Chuchundra, the musk-rat, who never comes out into the middle of the floor, but always creeps round by the wall, gave him advice, but Rikki-tikki did the real fighting.

2 He was a mongoose, rather like a little cat in his fur and his tail, but quite like a weasel in his head and his habits. His eyes and the end of his restless nose were pink. He could scratch himself anywhere he pleased with any leg, front or back, that he chose to use. He could fluff up his tail till it looked like a bottle brush, and his war cry as he scuttled through the long grass was: "Rikk-tikk-tikki-tikki-tchk!"

3 One day, a high summer flood washed him out of the burrow where he lived with his father and mother, and carried him, kicking and clucking, down a roadside ditch. He found a little wisp of grass floating there, and clung to it till he lost his senses. When he revived, he was lying in the hot sun on the middle of a garden path, very draggled indeed, and a small boy was saying, "Here's a dead mongoose. Let's have a funeral."

4 "No," said his mother, "let's take him in and dry him. Perhaps he isn't really dead."

5 They took him into the house, and a big man picked him up between his finger and thumb and said he was not dead but half choked. So they wrapped him in cotton wool, and warmed him over a little fire, and he opened his eyes and sneezed.

6 "Now," said the big man (he was an Englishman who had just moved into the bungalow), "don't frighten him, and we'll see what he'll do."

 2

⚙ Skill:
Textual Evidence

It says that he fluffs up his tail and he has a war cry. I know that a war cry is used in battle to rally the troops. This must mean that Rikki-tikki is brave and powerful, like a soldier.

⚙ Skill:
Text-Dependent
Responses

After finding Rikki-tikki, the English family brought him into their home and took care of him.

① Introduction

An Introduction to each text provides historical context for your reading as well as information about the author. You will also learn about the genre of the text and the year in which it was written.

② Notes

Many times, while working through the activities after each text, you will be asked to **annotate** or **make annotations** about what you are reading. This means that you should highlight or underline words in the text and use the "Notes" column to make comments or jot down any questions you have. You may also want to note any unfamiliar vocabulary words here.

You will also see sample student annotations to go along with the Skill lesson for that text.

 Reading & Writing
Companion

(3) First Read

During your first reading of each selection, you should just try to get a general idea of the content and message of the reading. Don't worry if there are parts you don't understand or words that are unfamiliar to you. You'll have an opportunity later to dive deeper into the text.

(4) Think Questions

These questions will ask you to start thinking critically about the text, asking specific questions about its purpose, and making connections to your prior knowledge and reading experiences. To answer these questions, you should go back to the text and draw upon specific evidence to support your responses. You will also begin to explore some of the more challenging vocabulary words in the selection.

(5) Skills

Each Skill includes two parts: Checklist and Your Turn. In the Checklist, you will learn the process for analyzing the text. The model student annotations in the text provide examples of how you might make your own notes following the instructions in the Checklist. In the Your Turn, you will use those same instructions to practice the skill.

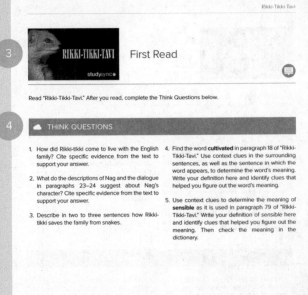

(3) RIKKI-TIKKI-TAVI studysync● First Read

Read "Rikki-Tikki-Tavi." After you read, complete the Think Questions below.

(4) ☁ THINK QUESTIONS

1. How did Rikki-tikki come to live with the English family? Cite specific evidence from the text to support your answer.

2. What do the descriptions of Nag and the dialogue in paragraphs 23–24 suggest about Nag's character? Cite specific evidence from the text to support your answer.

3. Describe in two to three sentences how Rikki-tikki saves the family from snakes.

4. Find the word **cultivated** in paragraph 18 of "Rikki-Tikki-Tavi." Use context clues in the surrounding sentences, as well as the sentence in which the word appears, to determine the word's meaning. Write your definition here and identify clues that helped you figure out the word's meaning.

5. Use context clues to determine the meaning of **sensible** as it is used in paragraph 79 of "Rikki-Tikki-Tavi." Write your definition of *sensible* here and identify clues that helped you figure out the meaning. Then check the meaning in the dictionary.

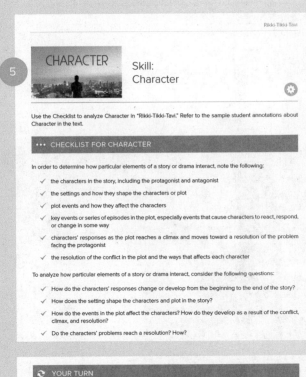

(5) CHARACTER sync●at.llp Skill: Character ⚙

Use the Checklist to analyze Character in "Rikki-Tikki-Tavi." Refer to the sample student annotations about Character in the text.

●●● CHECKLIST FOR CHARACTER

In order to determine how particular elements of a story or drama interact, note the following:

✓ the characters in the story, including the protagonist and antagonist

✓ the settings and how they shape the characters or plot

✓ plot events and how they affect the characters

✓ key events or series of episodes in the plot, especially events that cause characters to react, respond, or change in some way

✓ characters' responses as the plot reaches a climax and moves toward a resolution of the problem facing the protagonist

✓ the resolution of the conflict in the plot and the ways that affects each character

To analyze how particular elements of a story or drama interact, consider the following questions:

✓ How do the characters' responses change or develop from the beginning to the end of the story?

✓ How does the setting shape the characters and plot in the story?

✓ How do the events in the plot affect the characters? How do they develop as a result of the conflict, climax, and resolution?

✓ Do the characters' problems reach a resolution? How?

(5) ↻ YOUR TURN

1. How does the mother's love for her son affect her actions in paragraph 37?

○ A. It prompts her to keep her son away from Rikki-tikki.
○ B. It causes a disagreement between her and her husband.
○ C. It makes her show affection towards Rikki-tikki.
○ D. It makes Rikki-tikki feel nervous staying with the family.

2. What does the dialogue in paragraph 40 suggest about Chuchundra?

○ A. He is afraid.
○ B. He is easily fooled.
○ C. He is optimistic.
○ D. He loves Rikki-tikki.

3. Which paragraph shows that Teddy looks to Rikki-tikki for protection?

○ A. 37
○ B. 38
○ C. 39
○ D. 40

RIKKI-TIKKI-TAVI

studysync•

Close Read

Reread "Rikki-Tikki-Tavi." As you reread, complete the Skills Focus questions below. Then use your answers and annotations from the questions to help you complete the Write activity.

◎ SKILLS FOCUS

1. Identify details that reveal Nag's character when he is first introduced in the story. Explain what inferences you can make about Nag and what makes him a threat.

2. Identify details that reveal Rikki-tikki's character traits as a fighter. Explain how those character traits help Rikki-tikki defeat the snakes.

3. Find examples of Nag and Nagaina's actions and dialogue. How do their words and behaviors create conflict in the plot?

4. Identify details that help you compare and contrast Rikki-tikki and Darzee. Explain what you can infer about Rikki-tikki and Darzee from these details.

5. Analyze details that show how Rikki-tikki beats the snakes. Explain Rikki-tikki's approach to conflict.

✎ WRITE

LITERARY ANALYSIS: In this classic story of good vs. evil, Nag and Nagaina are portrayed as the villains. Consider the role and behaviors of the typical villain. Then think about Nag and Nagaina's behaviors, including how they impact the plot and interact with other characters. Do you think that Nag and Nagaina are truly evil, or have they been unfairly cast as villains? Choose a side, and write a brief response explaining your position and analysis. Use several pieces of textual evidence to support your points.

Ready for Marcos

FICTION

Introduction

Twelve-year-old Monica Alvarez has a happy life. She is a star on the track team and has many good friends. But everything changes when her parents bring Marcos, her new baby brother, home from the hospital. Her parents want her to have more responsibilities. Monica wonders what it will mean to be a big sister. Is she ready? Is she willing?

Ⓥ VOCABULARY

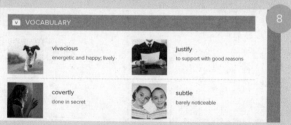

vivacious
energetic and happy; lively

justify
to support with good reasons

covertly
done in secret

subtle
barely noticeable

---

⑥ Close Read & Skills Focus

After you have completed the First Read, you will be asked to go back and read the text more closely and critically. Before you begin your Close Read, you should read through the Skills Focus to get an idea of the concepts you will want to focus on during your second reading. You should work through the Skills Focus by making annotations, highlighting important concepts, and writing notes or questions in the "Notes" column. Depending on instructions from your teacher, you may need to respond online or use a separate piece of paper to start expanding on your thoughts and ideas.

⑦ Write

Your study of each selection will end with a writing assignment. For this assignment, you should use your notes, annotations, personal ideas, and answers to both the Think and Skills Focus questions. Be sure to read the prompt carefully and address each part of it in your writing.

⑧ English Language Learner

The English Language Learner texts focus on improving language proficiency. You will practice learning strategies and skills in individual and group activities to become better readers, writers, and speakers.

Extended Writing Project and Grammar

This is your opportunity to use genre characteristics and craft to compose meaningful, longer written works exploring the theme of each unit. You will draw information from your readings, research, and own life experiences to complete the assignment.

1 Writing Project

After you have read all of the unit text selections, you will move on to a writing project. Each project will guide you through the process of writing your essay. Student models will provide guidance and help you organize your thoughts. One unit ends with an **Extended Oral Project,** which will give you an opportunity to develop your oral language and communication skills.

2 Writing Process Steps

There are four steps in the writing process: Plan, Draft, Revise, and Edit and Publish. During each step, you will form and shape your writing project, and each lesson's peer review will give you the chance to receive feedback from your peers and teacher.

3 Writing Skills

Each Skill lesson focuses on a specific strategy or technique that you will use during your writing project. Each lesson presents a process for applying the skill to your own work and gives you the opportunity to practice it to improve your writing.

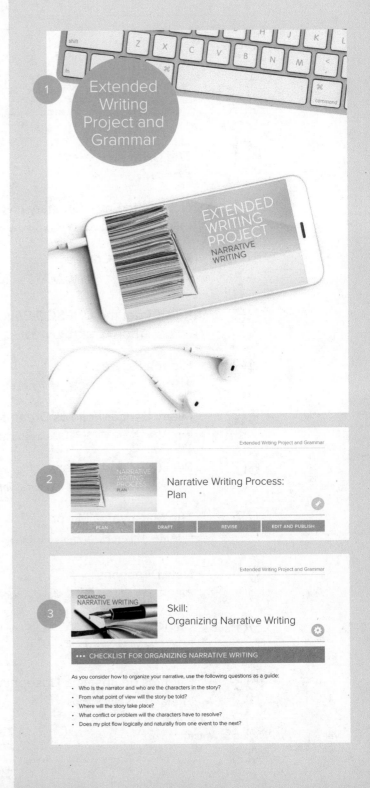

Extended Writing Project and Grammar

2 Narrative Writing Process: Plan

PLAN   DRAFT   REVISE   EDIT AND PUBLISH

Extended Writing Project and Grammar

3 Skill: Organizing Narrative Writing

••• CHECKLIST FOR ORGANIZING NARRATIVE WRITING

As you consider how to organize your narrative, use the following questions as a guide:

- Who is the narrator and who are the characters in the story?
- From what point of view will the story be told?
- Where will the story take place?
- What conflict or problem will the characters have to resolve?
- Does my plot flow logically and naturally from one event to the next?

The Power of One

How do we stand out from the crowd?

Genre Focus: DRAMA

Texts

 Paired Readings

Extended Oral Project and Grammar

How do we stand out from a crowd?

MAYA ANGELOU

Maya Angelou (1928–2014) was a poet, essayist, director, and playwright. Her most famous work is *I Know Why the Caged Bird Sings*, an autobiography. She was a member of the Harlem Writers Guild, where she met writer James Baldwin. She was the first black female director in Hollywood, and a Civil Rights activist who worked for Martin Luther King Jr. and Malcolm X. She was awarded the National Medal of the Arts in 2000 by President Bill Clinton, and the Presidential Medal of Freedom in 2011 by President Barack Obama.

LAURA BUSH

Former second-grade teacher and graduate of Southern Methodist University, Laura Lane Welch Bush (b. 1946) was born in Midland, Texas, earned her master's degree in library science from the University of Texas at Austin, and met her husband and future U.S. president George Walker Bush at a backyard barbecue at the home of mutual friends. As First Lady, she established the National Book Festival, was named by the United Nations as an honorary ambassador for the UN's Decade of LIteracy, and in 2002 was honored by the Elie Wiesel Foundation for Humanity.

NIKKI GIOVANNI

Born in Knoxville, Tennessee, poet Nikki Giovanni (b. 1943) graduated from Fisk University with honors in history, and since 1987 has served on the faculty at Virginia Tech, where she is a Distinguished Professor. She is the author of collections of poetry including *Black Feeling, Black Talk / Black Judgement;* and *Re: Creation*. She has received the Langston Hughes Award for Distinguished Contributions to Arts and Letters and the Rosa Parks Women of Courage Award. About her work, Giovanni has said, "Writing is . . . what I do to justify the air I breathe."

LOIS LOWRY

Newbery Medal-winning author Lois Lowry (b. 1937) was born in Honolulu, Hawaii, but relocated often following the path of her father's career in the military, which took her family from Japan to New York, Pennsylvania, California, and Connecticut. Lowry grew up dreaming of becoming a writer, and she found comfort in reading during a childhood of constant relocation. She graduated from the University of Southern Maine with a degree in English literature. Lowry's book *The Giver* has sold over 10 million copies and was adapted into a 2014 film.

KATHRYN SCHULTZ MILLER

Kathryn Schultz Miller is the cofounder of ArtReach Touring Theater, where she has also served as the Artistic Director for over twenty years. Miller is the recipient of a playwriting fellowship from the National Endowment for the Arts and the winner of the 1985 Post-Corbett Award "for literary excellence in playwriting." She is the author of fifty-six published plays, including *Haunted Houses* and *A Thousand Cranes*, which was performed at the Kennedy Center. Fourteen of her plays have been produced at the national level. She lives in Cincinnati.

GREGORY RAMOS

Gregory Ramos studied acting at Playwrights Horizons before earning his MFA in playwriting at UCLA. He has directed, written, and choreographed shows across the country, and served on the faculty of the University of Texas at El Paso, where he founded The Latino Guest Artists Program and the Border Public Theater. At the University of Vermont, he directed the Critical Race and Ethnic Studies Program. He currently teaches and serves as the chair of the school's Department of Theater, and is the board president of the Vermont Shakespeare Festival.

MARGOT LEE SHETTERLY

Long before Margot Lee Shetterly (b. 1969) wrote *Hidden Figures: The Story of the African-American Women Who Helped Win the Space Race*, her father worked as a research scientist at the NASA Langley Research Center. She grew up around other NASA families and later attended the University of Virginia. After pursuing a career in investment banking and launching a magazine in Mexico with her husband, she began research on *Hidden Figures*. The eventual 2016 film adaptation would be nominated for three Oscars and gross $236 million worldwide.

MEKEISHA MADDEN TOBY

Writer, editor, critic, journalist, and podcast producer Mekeisha Madden Toby has worked for the *Los Angeles Times, Variety*, CNN, *US Weekly*, espnW, and *Rotten Tomatoes*. Toby graduated with a degree in journalism from Wayne State University in Detroit, Michigan, where she grew up attending Cass Technical High School and working on her school newspaper. She currently hosts her own podcast, *TV Madness with Mekeisha Madden Toby*, which covers the film and television landscape, from Netflix to the big screen. Toby lives in Los Angeles.

BARBARA DEMICK

Barbara Demick began interviewing North Koreans for her future book *Nothing to Envy: Ordinary Lives in North Korea* starting in 2001, when her work for the *Los Angeles Times* brought her to Seoul, South Korea. For her reporting, Demick has won the Overseas Press Club's award, was named a finalist for the National Book Award, and was nominated for the Pulitzer Prize. The Ridgewood, New Jersey, native began her career with the *Philadelphia Inquirer,* when she lived in Sarajevo and worked as a foreign correspondent covering the Bosnian War from 1994–1996.

VELINA HASU HOUSTON

Playwright Velina Hasu Houston (b. 1957) was born in international waters on a military ship en route to the United States from Japan. She grew up in Junction City, Kansas, not far from the base to which her father was assigned, and attended both the University of California at Los Angeles and the University of Southern California. In 1991 she founded USC's Master of Fine Arts in Dramatic Writing program. She currently serves at USC as a Distinguished Professor, the first person of African descent to be named as such, and the Resident Playwright.

The Giver

FICTION
Lois Lowry
1993

Introduction

Lois Lowry (b. 1937) is a two-time Newbery Award winner for her novels *Number the Stars* and *The Giver*. A work of science fiction, *The Giver* focuses on Jonas's community, a place where there is no hunger, disease, or poverty, but also little individual choice. All major decisions are trusted to the Committee of Elders, and at age 12, each community member is assigned a career path by the Committee. In this excerpt, Jonas, who will soon turn 12, expresses his concerns

"The Ceremony of Twelve was the last of the Ceremonies. The most important."

Excerpt from Chapter 2

1 Jonas shivered. He pictured his father, who must have been a shy and quiet boy, for he was a shy and quiet man, seated with his group, waiting to be called to the stage. The Ceremony of Twelve was the last of the Ceremonies. The most important.

2 "I remember how proud my parents looked—and my sister, too; even though she wanted to be out riding the bicycle publicly, she stopped fidgeting and was very still and attentive when my turn came.

3 "But to be honest, Jonas," his father said, "for me there was not the **element** of suspense that there is with your Ceremony. Because I was already fairly certain of what my Assignment was to be."

4 Jonas was surprised. There was no way, really, to know in advance. It was a secret selection, made by the leaders of the community, the Committee of Elders, who took the responsibility so seriously that there were never even any jokes made about assignments.

5 His mother seemed surprised, too. "How could you have known?" she asked.

6 His father smiled his gentle smile. "Well, it was clear to me—and my parents later confessed that it had been obvious to them, too—what my **aptitude** was. I had always loved the newchildren more than anything. When my friends in my age group were holding bicycle races, or building toy vehicles or bridges with their construction sets, or—"

7 "All the things I do with my friends," Jonas pointed out, and his mother nodded in agreement.

8 "I always participated, of course, because as children we must experience all of those things. And I studied hard in school, just as you do, Jonas. But again and again, during free time, I found myself drawn to the newchildren. I spent almost all of my volunteer hours helping in the Nurturing Center. Of course the Elders knew that, from their observation."

Please note that excerpts and passages in the StudySync® library and this workbook are intended as touchstones to generate interest in an author's work. The excerpts and passages do not substitute for the reading of entire texts, and StudySync® strongly recommends that students seek out and purchase the whole literary or informational work in order to experience it as the author intended. Links to online resellers are available in our digital library. In addition, complete works may be ordered through an authorized reseller by filling out and returning to StudySync® the order form enclosed in this workbook.

Reading & Writing Companion   1

9   Jonas nodded. During the past year he had been aware of the increasing level of observation. In school, at recreation time, and during volunteer hours, he had noticed the Elders watching him and the other Elevens. He had seen them taking notes. He knew, too, that the Elders were meeting for long hours with all of the instructors that he and the other Elevens had had during their years of school.

10   "So I expected it, and I was pleased, but not at all surprised, when my Assignment was announced as **Nurturer**," Father explained.

11   "Did everyone applaud, even though they weren't surprised?" Jonas asked.

12   "Oh, of course. They were happy for me, that my Assignment was what I wanted most. I felt very fortunate." His father smiled.

13   "Were any of the Elevens disappointed, your year?" Jonas asked. Unlike his father, he had no idea what his Assignment would be. But he knew that some would disappoint him. Though he respected his father's work, Nurturer would not be his wish. And he didn't **envy** Laborers at all.

14   His father thought. "No, I don't think so. Of course the Elders are so careful in their observations and selections."

15   "I think it's probably the most important job in our community," his mother commented.

16   "My friend Yoshiko was surprised by her selection as Doctor," Father said, "but she was thrilled. And let's see, there was Andrei—I remember that when we were boys he never wanted to do physical things. He spent all the recreation time he could with his construction set, and his volunteer hours were always on building sites. The Elders knew that, of course. Andrei was given the Assignment of Engineer and he was delighted."

17   "Andrei later designed the bridge that crosses the river to the west of town," Jonas's mother said. "It wasn't there when we were children."

18   "There are very rarely disappointments, Jonas. I don't think you need to worry about that," his father reassured him. "And if there are, you know there's an **appeal** process." But they all laughed at that—an appeal went to a committee for study.

19   "I worry a little about Asher's Assignment," Jonas confessed. "Asher's such *fun*. But he doesn't really have any serious interests. He makes a game out of everything."

20   His father chuckled. "You know," he said, "I remember when Asher was a newchild at the Nurturing Center, before he was named. He never cried. He giggled and laughed at everything. All of us on the staff enjoyed nurturing Asher."

Copyright © BookheadEd Learning, LLC

21 "The Elders know Asher," his mother said. "They'll find exactly the right Assignment for him. I don't think you need to worry about him. But, Jonas, let me warn you about something that may not have occurred to you. I know I didn't think about it until after my Ceremony of Twelve."

22 "What's that?"

23 "Well, it's the last of the Ceremonies, as you know. After Twelve, age isn't important. Most of us even lose track of how old we are as time passes, though the information is in the Hall of Open Records, and we could go and look it up if we wanted to. What's important is the preparation for adult life, and the training you'll receive in your Assignment."

24 "I know that," Jonas said. "Everyone knows that."

25 "But it means," his mother went on, "that you'll move into a new group. And each of your friends will. You'll no longer be spending your time with your group of Elevens. After the Ceremony of Twelve, you'll be with your Assignment group, with those in training. No more volunteer hours. No more recreation hours. So your friends will no longer be as close."

26 Jonas shook his head. "Asher and I will always be friends," he said firmly. "And there will still be school."

27 "That's true," his father agreed. "But what your mother said is true as well. There will be changes."

28 *"Good* changes, though," his mother pointed out.

Excerpted from *The Giver* by Lois Lowry, published by Houghton Mifflin Harcourt.

✏ **WRITE**

PERSONAL RESPONSE: What do you think are the positive and negative aspects of living in a society in which each person's future occupation is decided for them? Would you want to live in such a society? Cite evidence from the text to support your response.

Please note that excerpts and passages in the StudySync® library and this workbook are intended as touchstones to generate interest in an author's work. The excerpts and passages do not substitute for the reading of entire texts, and StudySync® strongly recommends that students seek out and purchase the whole literary or informational work in order to experience it as the author intended. Links to online resellers are available in our digital library. In addition, complete works may be ordered through an authorized reseller by filling out and returning to StudySync® the order form enclosed in this workbook.

Reading & Writing Companion   3

Nothing to Envy:
Ordinary Lives in North Korea

INFORMATIONAL TEXT
Barbara Demick
2010

Introduction

n 2006, Barbara Demick won the Joe and Laurie Dine Award for Human Rights Reporting, and was named print journalist of the year by the Los Angeles Press Club. She received these accolades for her groundbreaking insight into the daily lives of North Koreans, who live under a totalitarian regime. In *Nothing to Envy*, Barbara Demick penetrates the shadowy dictatorship in order to share the lives of six ordinary individuals. The following excerpt features two of the main characters: Mrs. Song, a bookkeeper and loyal supporter of Kim Il-sung's regime, and her daughter Oak-hee, who is dangerously inclined to be skeptical. The excerpt begins with Mrs. Song and her husband Chang-bo, an independent thinker, watching television, an activity they proudly share with apartment house neighbors who cannot afford the luxury of TV.

"Spying on one's countrymen is something of a national pastime."

from Chapter Three: The True Believer

1. The program that got Chang-bo in trouble was an **innocuous** business report about a shoe factory producing rubber boots for the rainy season. The camera panned over crisply efficient workers on an assembly line where the boots were being produced by the thousands. The narrator raved about the superb quality of the boots and reeled off the impressive production statistics.

2. "Hah. If there are so many boots, how come my children never got any?" Chang-bo laughed aloud. The words tumbled out of his mouth before he could consider the consequences.

3. Mrs. Song never figured out which neighbor blabbed. Her husband's remark was quickly reported to the head of the *inminban*, the neighborhood watchdogs, who in turn passed on the information to the Ministry for the Protection of State Security. This **ominously** named agency is effectively North Korea's political police. It runs an extensive network of informers. By the accounts of **defectors**, there is at least one informer for every fifty people—more even than East Germany's notorious Stasi, whose files were pried open after German reunification.

4. Spying on one's countrymen is something of a national pastime. There were the young vigilantes from the Socialist Youth League like the one who stopped Mrs. Song for not wearing a badge. They also made sure people weren't violating the dress code by wearing blue jeans or T-shirts with Roman writing—considered a capitalist indulgence—or wearing their hair too long. The party issued regular edicts saying that men shouldn't allow the hair on top of their head to grow longer than five centimeters—though an exemption was granted for balding men, who were permitted seven centimeters. If a violation was severe, the offender could be arrested by the Public Standards Police. There were also *kyuch'aldae*, mobile police units who roamed the streets looking for offenders and had the right to barge into people's houses without notice. They would look for people who used more than their quota of electricity, a light bulb brighter than 40 watts, a hot plate, or a rice cooker. During one of the surprise inspections, one of the neighbors tried to hide their hot plate

Please note that excerpts and passages in the StudySync® library and this workbook are intended as touchstones to generate interest in an author's work. The excerpts and passages do not substitute for the reading of entire texts, and StudySync® strongly recommends that students seek out and purchase the whole literary or informational work in order to experience it as the author intended. Links to online resellers are available in our digital library. In addition, complete works may be ordered through an authorized reseller by filling out and returning to StudySync® the order form enclosed in this workbook.

Reading & Writing Companion

5

under a blanket and ended up setting their apartment on fire. The mobile police often dropped in after midnight to see if there were any overnight guests who might have come to visit without travel permits. It was a serious offense, even if it was just an out-of-town relative, and much worse if the guest happened to be a lover. But it wasn't just the police and the volunteer leagues who did the snooping. Everybody was supposed to be vigilant for subversive behavior and transgressions of the rules. Since the country was too poor and the power supply too unreliable for electronic surveillance, state security relied on human intelligence—snitches[1]. The newspapers would occasionally run feature stories about heroic children who ratted out their parents. To be denounced by a neighbor for bad-mouthing the **regime** was nothing extraordinary.

5   Chang-bo's interrogation lasted three days. The agents yelled and cursed at him, although they never beat him—at least that's what he told his wife. He claimed afterward that his gift with language helped him talk his way out of the bind. He cited the truth in his defense.

6   "I wasn't insulting anybody. I was simply saying that I haven't been able to buy those boots and I'd like to have some for my family," Chang-bo protested indignantly.

7   He made a convincing case. He was a commanding figure with his potbelly and his stern expression. He looked like the epitome of a Workers' Party official. The political police in the end decided not to push the case and released him without charges.

8   When he returned home, he got a tongue-lashing from his wife that was almost harsher than the interrogation. It was the worst fight of their marriage. For Mrs. Song, it was not merely that her husband had been disrespectful of the government; for the first time in her life, she felt the stirrings of fear. Her conduct had always been so impeccable and her **devotion** so genuine that it never occurred to her that she might be vulnerable.

9   "Why did you say such nonsense when there were neighbors in the apartment? Didn't you realize you could have jeopardized everything we have?" she railed at him.

10   In fact, they both realized how lucky they were. If not for Chang-bo's excellent class background and his party membership, he would not have been let off so lightly. It helped, too, that Mrs. Song had at various times been head of the *inminban* in the building and commanded some respect from the state security officers. Chang-bo's offhand remark was precisely the kind of thing

---

1. **snitches** informers

that could result in deportation to a prison camp in the mountains if the offender didn't have a solid position in the community. They had heard of a man who cracked a joke about Kim Jong-il's height and was sent away for life. Mrs. Song personally knew a woman from her factory who was taken away for something she wrote in her diary. At the time, Mrs. Song hadn't felt any pity for the woman. "The traitor probably deserved what she got," she'd said to herself. Now she felt embarrassed for having thought such a thing.

11 The incident seemed to blow over. Chastened by the experience, Chang-bo was more careful about what he said outside the family, but his thoughts were running wild. For many years, Chang-bo had been fighting off the doubts that would periodically creep into his consciousness. Now those doubts were gelling into outright disbelief. As a journalist, Chang-bo had more access to information than ordinary people. At the North Hamgyong Provincial Broadcasting Company, where he worked, he and his colleagues heard uncensored news reports from the foreign media. It was their job to sanitize it for domestic consumption. Anything positive that happened in capitalist countries or especially South Korea, which in 1988 hosted the Summer Olympics, was downplayed. Strikes, disasters, riots, murders—elsewhere— got plenty of coverage.

12 Chang-bo's job was to report business stories. He toured collective farms, shops, and factories with a notebook and tape recorder, interviewing the managers. Back in the newsroom, he would write his stories in fountain pen (there were no typewriters) about how well the economy was doing. He always put a positive spin on the facts, although he tried to keep them at least plausible. By the time they were edited by his superiors in Pyongyang, however, any glimmer of the truth was gone. Chang-bo knew better than anyone that the supposed triumphs of the North Korean economy were **fabrications.** He had good reason to scoff at the report about the rubber boots.

13 He had one trusted friend from the radio station who shared his increasing disdain for the regime. When the two of them got together, Chang-bo would open a bottle of Mrs. Song's *neungju* and, after a few drinks, they would let rip their true feelings.

14 "What a bunch of liars!" Chang-bo would say in an emphatic tone, taking care just the same not to speak loudly enough for the sound to carry through the thin plaster walls between the apartments.

15 "Crooks, all of them."

Please note that excerpts and passages in the StudySync® library and this workbook are intended as touchstones to generate interest in an author's work. The excerpts and passages do not substitute for the reading of entire texts, and StudySync® strongly recommends that students seek out and purchase the whole literary or informational work in order to experience it as the author intended. Links to online resellers are available in our digital library. In addition, complete works may be ordered through an authorized reseller by filling out and returning to StudySync® the order form enclosed in this workbook.

Reading & Writing Companion   7

NOTES

16   "The son is even worse than the father."

17   Oak-hee eavesdropped on her father and his friend. She nodded quietly in agreement. When her father noticed, he at first tried to shoo her away. Eventually he gave up. Swearing her to secrecy, he took her into his confidence. He told her that Kim Il-sung was not the anti-Japanese resistance fighter he claimed to be so much as a puppet of the Soviet Union. He told her that South Korea was now among the richest countries in Asia; even ordinary working people owned their own cars. Communism, he reported, was proving a failure as an economic system. China and the Soviet Union were now embracing capitalism. Father and daughter would talk for hours, always taking care to keep their voices at a whisper in case a neighbor was snooping around. And, at such times, they always made sure that Mrs. Song, the true believer, was not at home.

Excerpted from *Nothing to Envy: Ordinary Lives in North Korea* by Barbara Demick, published by Spiegel & Grau

---

✏ WRITE

PERSONAL RESPONSE: Imagine that you are a journalist and want to write an article explaining to someone why it is so dangerous to speak freely in North Korea. Write an article explaining the challenges concerning people's use of free speech, incorporating examples and information from the text.

A Thousand Cranes

DRAMA
Kathryn Schultz Miller
1990

Introduction

Kathryn Schultz Miller is a playwright and the winner of the 1985 Post-Corbett Award for "literary excellence in playwriting." She served as co-founder and artistic director of ArtReach Touring Theatre based in Cincinnati. Among her produced works are *Island Son*, *The Legend of Sleepy Hollow*, and *Amelia Hart*. *A Thousand Cranes* is based on a true story of a young Japanese girl named Sadako Sasaki who was two years old when the atomic bombs were dropped on Hiroshima and Nagasaki on August 6th and August 9th during the final stages of World War II. At twelve she became ill with "radiation sickness." As she hoped to get better, she attempted to fold a thousand cranes.

"I wished that there will never ever be a bomb like that again."

Skill: Dramatic Elements and Structure

At first, the music is gentle and pleasant. Then when the actors start counting, the stage directions say that there is percussion. This gives the play an urgent tone. The form of this play is probably tragedy.

The music and the percussion all build to Sadako's monologue. I know she has an important story to tell.

1   AT RISE: *The playing area is a circle of about 20 feet by 20 feet. Audience is seated on three sides of the playing area. Upstage R of the circle will be a musical or instrument "station" with percussion instruments and recorded music arranged in such a way that at* **appropriate** *times actors may sit comfortably on a stool and contribute music and sound effects to the performance. UL are standing fans of various pastels and varying heights, the tallest being less than 5 feet. To the left and right downstage are two white masks on each side in tube holders about waist high. GRANDMOTHER OBA CHAN will wear a magnificent Japanese mask. ACTORS 1 and 2 will carry white masks when playing the parts of the DOCTORS. SPIRITS will be indicated by red masks on holders but will not actually be worn by actors. SADAKO, KENJI, MOTHER and FATHER will not wear masks. ACTORS 1 and 2 will wear all black. SADAKO wears a* **simple** *western-style school uniform of a skirt and a blouse with a tie.*

2   *The play begins in silence. ACTORS 1 and 2 bow to each other before the music stand. SADAKO watches from behind the music stand. ACTORS 1 and 2 mime lifting a large piece of paper off the floor. In mirrored motions, they carry the paper to DC, carefully place it on the floor and gently smooth it out. They bow again, then turn U. SADAKO crosses down to paper as recorded folding music begins. The mood of the music gentle and pleasant. ACTORS 1 and 2 count with SADAKO as she mimes the folding of a larger-than-life crane.*

3   ALL *(punctuating their words with percussion sounds).* One, two, three, four, five, six, seven, eight, nine . . . *(SADAKO mimes the lifting of the giant bird with both hands. It is very light. She thrusts the bird into flight.)*

4   SADAKO. Ten. *(SADAKO blows as if to launch it. ALL watch it in the sky, from left to right. TO AUDIENCE.)* My name is Sadako. I was born in Japan in 1943. My home was called Hiroshima. *(Quiet sound effects come from ACTORS 1 and 2.)* When I was two years old, my mother held me in her arms. She sang a song to me. *(ACTOR 2 sings in a soothing, quiet melody.)* It was a quiet summer morning. Inside our small house my Grandmother was preparing tea. *(SADAKO pauses while ACTOR 2 sings.)* Suddenly there was a tremendous flash of light that cut across the sky! *(A very, very loud startling BOOM noise.*

Copyright © BookheadEd Learning, LLC

SADAKO falls into a kneeling position, covering her head. When all is quiet she stands.) My name is Sadako. This is my story. *(A dramatic rhythm beat, not as loud as before and slowly fading.)*

5   ACTOR 2 *(quietly fading away).* Sixty-seven, sixty-eight, sixty-nine, seventy...

6   *(SADAKO and ACTOR 1, now KENJI, have moved U and now KENJI comes bounding on to playing area, out of breath and laughing. He wears a black cap to distinguish himself as KENJI. He begins to count, determining by how many seconds he has won the race with SADAKO. As ACTOR 2's counting fades he picks it up. They say the primary numbers, one and two and three, etc., together.)*

7   ACTOR 2 *(fading).* Seventy . . . seventy-one . . . seventy-two . . .

8   KENJI. One . . . two . . . three . . . four

9   *(SADAKO runs in out of breath and laughing.)*

10 KENJI. Beat you by four seconds.

11 SADAKO. Four? You're lying!

12 KENJI *(laughing).* It was actually four and a half, but I let you have that.

13 SADAKO. Oh! You . . . ! *(Slumping.)* You always win! You should let somebody else win sometime.

14 KENJI. Why, Sadako. You can't mean that I should cheat so that you can win.

15 SADAKO. Oh, it wouldn't be cheating so much as . . . polite.

16 KENJI *(laughing).* And I suppose when you run in the girl's contest next month you'll want the judges to be *polite* and let somebody else win.

17 SADAKO. Well, no.

18 KENJI. I thought so.

19 SADAKO. Oh, Kenji, do you think I have a chance to win?

20 KENJI *(mocking).* You? You win a race against the fastest girls in Hiroshima? You can't win.

21 SADAKO. Why not?

NOTES

Skill:
Character

I know from the stage directions that this story will be about Sadako. She will probably be the protagonist. I think this is interesting because the play starts with her explaining the bombing of Hiroshima. I wonder if the bomb had any effect on her? She seems happy and loves to race and win. I wonder if the contest will be important in this play. How will it impact Sadako and the plot?

22 KENJI. Because you're a turtle, that's why. A great big lumbering turtle. *(Mimes slow turtle, laughing at his jest.)*

23 SADAKO. I am not a turtle.

24 KENJI. Yes, you are.

25 SADAKO. Am not.

26 KENJI. Are too.

27 SADAKO. Well, if I'm a turtle, then you're a frog!

28 KENJI. A frog?

29 SADAKO. Yes. A great big green one with warts all over it.

30 KENJI. Sadako, you can't possibly mean . . . croak . . . *(Putting her on.)* Well, where on earth could that have come from? Croak!

31 SADAKO. Oh, you.

32 KENJI. Look, Sadako, my hand is turning green . . . croak . . . and it has warts all over it! *(He crouches to a frog position and sticks out his tongue, leaping around, croaking. Uses bill of his cap to indicate the mouth of the croaking frog.)* Croak! Croak!

33 SADAKO *(laughing in spite of herself).* Now, you stop that. *(She is laughing almost uncontrollably; soon KENJI stops and laughs with her. They stop, leaning on each other, gaining composure.)* Kenji, tell me the truth. Do you think I have *any* chance of winning the races next month?

34 KENJI. Sadako, I will tell you the truth. I believe you will win.

35 SADAKO *(thrilled).* You really think so? You really, really do?

36 KENJI. Yes. I really, really do.

37 SADAKO. Oh, Kenji! *(She hugs him.)* Wait until I tell my father. He will be so proud of me! *(She starts to go.)*

38 KENJI. Now don't quit practicing!

39 SADAKO. Oh, I won't.

Copyright © BookheadEd Learning, LLC

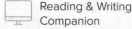

40   KENJI. See you tomorrow?

41   SADAKO. Tomorrow! *(She moves U as if to exit.)*

42   *(KENJI, now ACTOR 1, moves to instrument station and makes music for scene change. SADAKO moves U as ACTOR 2, now MOTHER, moves into the scene. She is counting out candles and putting them on the table. She wears a kimono. ACTOR 1 counts and then fades as MOTHER joins in and finally ends the counting.)*

43   ACTOR 1. One hundred and eighteen, one hundred and nineteen, one hundred and twenty, one hundred and twenty-one, one hundred and twenty-two . . . one hundred and twenty-three . . . *(Again, they speak the primary numbers together.)*

44   MOTHER *(counting candles)*. One . . . two . . . three . . . four . . .

45   *(SADAKO comes running in, very excited.)*

46   SADAKO. Mother, Mother! Wait till you hear! I have wonderful news!

47   MOTHER *(not looking up, continues working)*. Your shoes, Sadako.

48   SADAKO. Oh. *(She calms down to **remove** her shoes, puts them by the door, then rushes back to MOTHER.)* Wait till I tell you!

49   MOTHER. Sadako, show your respect to your elders.

50   SADAKO. Oh. *(She bows, puts hands together as in prayer and bows her head toward MOTHER.)* Mother, Kenji just told me . . . !

51   MOTHER. Sadako, show your respect to our beloved ancestors. *(Disheartened, SADAKO kneels before an imaginary shrine, hands in prayer and bowing her head. Returns to MOTHER, somewhat **subdued**.)*

52   SADAKO. Mother, I . . .

53   MOTHER. You must wait for your father to tell this earth-shattering news. Now it is time to prepare for dinner.

54   SADAKO. But, Mother . . .

55   MOTHER. Sushi has been prepared, the rice plates have been set. Sadako, you may warm the saki for your father.

56 SADAKO. Yes, Mother. *(MOTHER straightens candles on the table.)*

57 *(FATHER enters, takes off his shoes.)*

58 SADAKO. Father! *(She runs to him, grabs him in embrace and almost twirls him around.)* Wait till I tell you!

59 FATHER. Well, what is this?

60 MOTHER *(not angry).* This daughter of yours will not learn **discipline.**

61 FATHER. Your mother is right, Sadako. You must learn moderation in all things.

62 SADAKO. But, Father. I have such wonderful news!

63 FATHER *(warm).* It seems that everything in your world is wonderful, Sadako. *(Kisses the top of her head.)* You may tell us your news.

64 SADAKO *(looks anxiously at them BOTH).* Now?

65 FATHER *(laughing).* Now, Sadako.

66 SADAKO. Kenji says I'm fast enough to win the race next month! Isn't that wonderful? He thinks I can *win!*

67 FATHER *(genuinely impressed).* You have been practicing very hard.

68 SADAKO. Oh, yes, Father. Kenji and I run every day.

69 FATHER. Kenji is a fast runner, an excellent athlete.

70 SADAKO. Yes, he is, Father. And a good teacher too.

71 MOTHER. Even so, you must use discipline to practice very hard if you really want to win.

72 SADAKO. Oh, I want to win, Mother. I want to win more than anything on earth!

73 FATHER. We are very proud of you, Sadako. *(BOTH parents hug her. MOTHER begins to light candles.)*

74 SADAKO. Mother, why are you lighting candles on the table?

75 MOTHER. Soon it will be Oban, Sadako.

76   FATHER. It is the day of the spirits.

77   MOTHER. We light a candle for our ancestors who have died.

78   FATHER. We ask them to return to us and join in our celebration of life.

79   MOTHER *(has lit all but last candle)*. This one is for Oba chan, your Grandmother.

80   SADAKO. I remember her. I was only a baby, but I remember how warm my grandmother's hands were. *(She kneels before the candles. MOTHER and FATHER move away. Their lines now sound like statements in a dream.)*

81   FATHER. Oba chan died in the Thunderbolt.

82   SADAKO. She had a gentle voice.

83   MOTHER. Suddenly there was a great flash of light.

84   SADAKO. Her smile was like sunshine.

85   FATHER. It cut through the sky!

86   SADAKO. Grandmother? Grandmother?

87   MOTHER. The world was filled with blinding light. *(MOTHER and FATHER spin away with arms up in protecting gesture. They twirl to their places behind the music stand where they make percussion sounds.)*

88   SADAKO. Can you hear me, Grandmother?

89   FATHER. It took our friends.

90   SADAKO. Can your spirit really return like they say?

91   MOTHER. It took our home.

92   SADAKO. Are you watching me now? Do you see me when I run?

93   FATHER. It took your Grandmother, Oba chan.

94   *(MOTHER and FATHER now become ACTOR 1 and ACTOR 2. They use a percussion sound that builds and when it stops the silence is startling. They begin to count.)*

95   ACTORS 1 and 2. One hundred and fifty-one . . .

NOTES

96   SADAKO. One. *(Blows out first candle.)*

97   ACTORS 1 and 2. One hundred and fifty-two . . .

98   SADAKO. Two. *(Blows out second candle.)*

99   ACTORS 1 and 2. One hundred and fifty-three . . .

100   SADAKO. Three. *(Blows out third candle.)*

101   ACTORS 1 and 2. One hundred and fifty-four . . .

102   SADAKO *(before the candle of her GRANDMOTHER, looks up)*. Will I win my race, Grandmother? Can you hear me now? *(Turns back to candle.)* Four. *(Blows out candle, stands and looks around.)* Grandmother?

103   *(ACTOR 1 plays a loud dramatic percussion sound that fades. ACTOR 2, using the voice she will use later as GRANDMOTHER, speaks.)*

104   ACTOR 2/GRANDMOTHER *(as she moves slowly, twirling away until she is hidden behind the largest fan)*. I hear you, Sadako!

105   *(The loud cymbal¹ sound comes again and fades into a new sound. Now a fast, quick staccato² sound is heard from the instrument stand. ACTOR 1 also is KENJI, using only the voice from his location. ACTOR 2 turns U to put on GRANDMOTHER OBA CHAN's mask. SADAKO begins to run in place.)*

106   KENJI *(moving D to replace set piece and back to music stand.)* You little turtle, you'll never win at that speed. *(SADAKO speaks as if he is beside her, running.)*

107   SADAKO *(running)*. I am not a turtle!

108   KENJI. Sure you are, that's how fast turtles run, isn't it?

109   SADAKO. Croak, croak, croak! *(They BOTH laugh.)*

110   KENJI. I bet I can make it to the river before you!

111   SADAKO. Bet you can't.

112   KENJI. Bet I can!

---

1. **cymbal** a brass plate that makes a ringing or clashing sound when struck
2. **staccato** (in music) consisting of sharp, separate notes

113 SADAKO. Bet you can't. *(She runs faster in place as percussion sound also speeds up.)*

114 *(ACTOR 2, who now becomes GRANDMOTHER OBA CHAN, turns and raises her arms. Her costume and mask are magnificent. A majestic sound is used by ACTOR 1 to accompany her movement. SADAKO is becoming out of breath. GRANDMOTHER makes a magical gesture toward SADAKO. SADAKO trips and falls.)*

115 KENJI *(still out of scene)*. Sadako, are you alright?

116 SADAKO *(rubbing her hip)*. Oooh . . .

117 KENJI. Here, let me help you up. *(She takes his imaginary hand and stands.)* Are you all right?

118 SADAKO. Yes, I'm fine.

119 KENJI. All right then, let's begin again. *(Again, SADAKO runs very fast to the music. Again, GRANDMOTHER makes her magical gesture. SADAKO falls.)* Sadako?

120 SADAKO. I'm okay. Just a little dizzy, that's all. *(Staccato music begins again very fast, but SADAKO is slowing down.)*

121 KENJI. Discipline, Sadako! *(She speeds up; we can see that she is in pain but she picks up the pace of the run.)*

122 SADAKO. I'm trying, Grandmother. I want to win, Grandmother. I want to fly like the wind!

123 GRANDMOTHER/ACTOR 2. I hear you, Sadako! *(SADAKO moves slowly in a circle, obviously dizzy.)*

124 *(KENJI and GRANDMOTHER become ACTORS 1 and 2. During the following lines, masks on poles will be carried and moved in the air by ACTORS 1 and 2. The masks will be stark white and ghostly. ACTORS 1 and 2 may use many voices and the lines should run into each other to give the impression of many. SADAKO tries to escape the floating faces but they dance around her, bearing down to force her to bed. Recorded music uses a gong sound and heavy beat.)*

125 ACTOR 1. What is the matter with Sadako?

126 ACTOR 2. What is the matter with Sadako?

NOTES

127 ACTOR 1. Why did she fall?

128 ACTOR 2. Why did she fall?

129 ACTOR 1. What could be wrong?

130 ACTOR 2. What could be wrong?

131 SADAKO. Nothing! I'm just tired, that's all!

132 ACTOR 1. X-ray her chest.

133 ACTOR 2. Examine her blood.

134 ACTOR 1. Put her in a hospital.

135 ACTORS 1 and 2. Hospital, hospital, hospital . . .

136 SADAKO. A hospital? No!

137 ACTOR 1. Put her to bed.

138 ACTOR 2. Put her to bed.

139 SADAKO. But there's nothing wrong with me!

140 ACTOR 1. Why did she fall?

141 ACTOR 2. Why did she fall?

142 ACTOR 1. Take some more tests.

143 ACTOR 2. Take some more tests.

144 ACTOR 1. You'll be just fine.

145 ACTOR 2. Now don't you worry.

146 ACTOR 1. Don't you worry.

147 ACTOR 2. Put her to bed.

148 SADAKO. But I'll miss the race!

149 ACTOR 1. Now don't you worry.

NOTES

150   ACTOR 2. You'll be just fine.

151   ACTOR 1. Put her to bed.

152   SADAKO. I want to fly like the wind!

153   ACTORS 1 and 2 *(holding white masks above their stands)*. Leukemia[3], leukemia, leukemia, leukemia, leukemia, leukemia . . .

154   SADAKO. Leukemia?

155   *(ACTORS 1 and 2 drop masks into holders with a jarring thud. They become MOTHER and FATHER speaking with faces forward as if speaking to a doctor.)*

156   MOTHER. Leukemia? My little girl? But that's impossible! The atom bomb didn't even do so much as scratch her!

157   FATHER. The atom-bomb sickness? My daughter?

158   SADAKO. But it can't be true, Mother, can it? *(MOTHER and FATHER rush to her seated on the bench.)* I don't have any scars from the bomb. It didn't touch me. It can't be true, can it, Mother?

159   FATHER. There now, dear, they just want to do some more tests.

160   SADAKO. But how can I be sick from the bomb? It killed my grandmother but I wasn't hurt at all.

161   MOTHER *(very gently)*. Sadako, the radiation[4] doesn't always show up right away.

162   SADAKO *(terrified)*. I was only two when the bomb fell.

163   FATHER. It's just a few tests, that's all, sweetheart.

164   MOTHER. You'll be here a few weeks.

165   SADAKO. But the race . . . *(MOTHER and FATHER are fighting back tears.)*

166   MOTHER. We'll be back every day to see you. *(Rushes off to hide tears, to music stand.)*

---

3. **leukemia** a cancer in which the bone marrow and other blood-forming organs produce increased numbers of white blood cells and suppress the production of normal blood cells
4. **radiation** an effect of nuclear reactions, usually in the form of particles or electromagnetic waves

Skill: Dramatic Elements and Structure

The drumming makes things feel urgent again. I wonder if something important is about to happen in the plot.

The actors are all counting with Sadako. This makes me think that her story is bigger than just Sadako. The play must be building up to a larger message for the community or society.

167 FATHER. Get some rest, sweetheart. *(Kisses her. Exits to music stand.)*

168 SADAKO. The race . . .

169 *(ACTOR 1 prepares to become KENJI. Using the instruments to punctuate her lines, ACTOR 2 counts.)*

170 ACTOR 2. Two hundred and thirty-four, two hundred and thirty-five, two hundred and thirty-six, two hundred and thirty-seven . . . *(The counting fades and SADAKO counts. Again, the primary numbers are spoken together by ACTORS 1 and 2 and SADAKO.)*

171 SADAKO. Six, seven, eight, nine, ten . . .

172 *(KENJI enters the scene.)*

173 KENJI. What are you counting?

174 SADAKO *(sees him, delighted)*. Oh, Kenji, I'm so glad you're here! *(They embrace.)*

175 KENJI. What's so interesting out there?

176 SADAKO. I am counting how many trees I can see from my window. This morning I counted the flowers. There were fifty-two. You know, it's only been ten years since the bomb destroyed everything. But look how many trees have grown since then!

177 KENJI. I have a present for you.

178 SADAKO. You do?

179 KENJI. Close your eyes. *(She squinches them very tight. KENJI puts a piece of gold paper on the bed and some scissors.)* Now you can look.

180 SADAKO *(looking at paper)*. What is it?

181 KENJI *(laughs)*. I've figured out a way for you to get well. Watch! *(He slowly folds paper into origami crane. Recorded music used earlier in the mimed folding is heard. He holds the crane in the palm of his hand as if it is very precious and holds it out to SADAKO.)*

182 SADAKO. Kenji, it's beautiful. *(Takes crane.)* But how can this paper crane make me well?

183   KENJI. Don't you remember that old story about the crane? It's supposed to live for a thousand years. If a sick person folds one thousand paper cranes, the gods will grant her wish and make her healthy again. There's your first one.

184   SADAKO *(very touched)*. Oh, Kenji, it's beautiful.

185   KENJI. Make a wish. *(The magical sound of chimes is heard from the music stand. SADAKO holds it out before her, closes her eyes, and her lips move silently. She looks up to KENJI, very moved by his gift.)*

186   SADAKO. Thank you, Kenji. Thank you.

187   KENJI. Don't thank me. You have to fold the rest yourself.

188   SADAKO. I'll start today. *(Looks around.)* But I'll need paper.

189   KENJI *(putting her on)*. Now where in the world could we get some paper? *(Pretends to think, then pulls some out of his satchel.)* Well, what do you know? Look what I have here. *(Hands it to her.)* This ought to keep you busy.

190   SADAKO *(takes the paper, smiles at his fun, becomes serious)*. Kenji?

191   KENJI. Yes?

192   SADAKO *(trying to be strong)*. Who won the race?

193   KENJI *(carefully)*. Oh, I don't remember her name. She wasn't very fast. She was a turtle.

194   SADAKO. But you always said *I* was a turtle.

195   KENJI. Oh, well, I was only teasing when I said that. You're more like that crane there. You run very fast, Sadako, like a bird. Like the wind.

196   SADAKO *(almost ready to cry, bolsters herself)*. So if I'm not a turtle, does that mean you're not a frog?

197   KENJI. What? Me? A frog. Why, that's the silliest thing I ever heard . . . Croak! Oops! There's that sound again. Croak! Uh-oh. It's starting again, Sadako. Look! Croak! I'm turning all green and warty! Croak! Croak! *(He continues to play the frog until SADAKO is laughing helplessly.)*

198   *(A percussion sound bridges the scene into transition. ALL count together. ACTOR 1 brings bough of paper cranes to SADAKO, moves back to music stand. ACTORS 1 and 2 fade away and become MOTHER and FATHER.*

NOTES

SADAKO continues counting. She is holding a very long rope of colorful paper cranes.)

199 ACTORS 1 and 2 and SADAKO. Four hundred and thirty-two, four hundred and thirty-three, four hundred and thirty-four, four hundred and thirty-five . . .

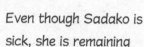

Skill:
Character

Even though Sadako is sick, she is remaining positive and hopeful. I can tell that her energy and attitude are encouraging her parents and making them happy, too! Her friends are still important to her, especially Kenji, and her relationship with him is helping her remain positive and hopeful. Will her positive energy last?

200 SADAKO (*cheerful, counting cranes*). Four hundred and thirty-six, four hundred and thirty-seven, four hundred and thirty-eight!

201 *(She holds them up for MOTHER and FATHER who have just entered.)*

202 SADAKO. See. (*MOTHER and FATHER are very pleased to see her so happy and energetic.*) Kenji taught me! You shouldn't worry about me anymore. Kenji figured out a way for me to get well. Do you remember the story? If a sick person folds a thousand paper cranes then the gods will make her well again. And look. I've already folded four hundred and thirty-eight! *(She holds them up, proud and delighted, full of new vigor.)*

203 MOTHER. Oh, I'm so glad. I thought you would be sad about not being able to run in the races.

204 SADAKO (*trying to hide her sudden sadness*). Oh, that. Oh, I don't think about that old race anymore. Silly old race. What good was it? Kenji said I was better than the girl who ran. He said I run like a bird. It's like I'm flying, he said. Folding cranes is much better than any old race. (*MOTHER and FATHER glance at each other.*) It's kind of like a race anyway, don't you think? If I fold them fast enough I won't have to die. (*SADAKO smiles radiantly at her parents. Her MOTHER gasps and grabs SADAKO, pressing her daughter's head against her breast, and cries. Pause. MOTHER and FATHER move away, leaving SADAKO alone. She is asleep and speaks with her eyes closed.*) Mother? Mother, where are you? Father? Oh, just you wait, Father. I'll make you so proud of me! I'm going to win. I'm going to win! Oh, but Mother! Father? Where are you now? I don't like it here. It's lonely and I don't feel well. It hurts. It HURTS!!

205 *(ACTORS 1 and 2 become DOCTORS and enter the scene.)*

206 ACTOR 1. What's the matter with Sadako?

207 ACTOR 2. What's the matter with Sadako?

208 ACTOR 1. Why did she fall?

209 ACTOR 2. What could be wrong?

210 ACTOR 1. Put her to bed.

211 ACTOR 2. Put her to bed.

212 SADAKO. No, I don't want to stay in bed!

213 ACTOR 1. Now don't you worry.

214 ACTOR 2. You'll be just fine.

215 SADAKO. But it hurts! And I have such bad dreams.

216 ACTORS 1 and 2. Put her to bed. Put her to bed. Put her to bed. Put her to bed. *(They repeat as they move away, their voices fading to a whisper.)*

217 SADAKO. Grandmother? Grandmother? Can you see me? Can you hear me now?

218 *(There is a dramatic percussion sound from ACTOR 1 as ACTOR 2 dons her magnificent GRANDMOTHER mask and enters the scene. She makes a grand entrance with beautiful recorded music and chimes.)*

219 GRANDMOTHER. I hear you, Sadako.

220 SADAKO *(slowly opens her eyes, pause, sees GRANDMOTHER)*. Grandmother! You came back! You returned to earth just like they said.

221 GRANDMOTHER. Yes, I have returned to help you, Sadako.

222 SADAKO. Oh, Grandmother, I hurt so much! It's so cold and lonely here. Can I go home now?

223 GRANDMOTHER *(beckoning)*. I have come to show you something. Come.

224 SADAKO. Oh, I wish I could go with you, Grandmother.

225 GRANDMOTHER. I will take you to the mountains and rivers of our ancestors.

226 SADAKO. Oh, but, Grandmother, how can I go with you? They won't even let me leave my room. They say I have to stay in bed.

227 GRANDMOTHER. You know a way.

228 SADAKO. I do?

229 *(GRANDMOTHER stands stoically as ACTOR 1 brings imagined piece of paper downstage as before. He gently smoothes it on the floor before SADAKO, bows, and moves upstage again.)*

NOTES

230 SADAKO. Of course. Yes, now I know.

231 *(SADAKO performs the mimed folding of a giant crane. This is a kind of choreographed dance that was used in the introduction. The "folding" is accompanied by specific music used in each folding sequence. GRANDMOTHER moves with SADAKO as she folds in a way that suggests she is directing SADAKO. When the folding is complete, GRANDMOTHER and SADAKO look at each other, then slowly move down to lift the crane together. As they stoop to pick up the crane, a dramatic music with gong sound begins. They carry the crane to bench, SADAKO on left side, GRANDMOTHER on right. They place bench/crane C. GRANDMOTHER stands on bench behind her and ACTOR 1 stands on floor with back to AUDIENCE behind GRANDMOTHER. A whooshing sound is heard as ACTORS contract together to suggest the launching of the bird into flight. ACTOR 1 uses mylar streamers[5] to "flap" elegantly as wings. SADAKO is thrilled. ACTOR 1 counts loud and dramatically, indicating the excitement of the moment. Loud, beautiful, fast-paced music accompanies their glorious flight.)*

232 ACTOR 1. Five hundred and sixty-three, five hundred and sixty-four, five hundred and sixty-five!

233 SADAKO *(thrilled).* Look, Grandmother, it's just like Kenji said. I fly like the wind! I fly like the wind!

234 ACTOR 1. Five hundred and seventy-one! Five hundred and seventy-two! FIVE HUNDRED AND SEVENTY-THREE!!!

235 SADAKO. I FLY LIKE THE WIND!! *(ACTOR 1 moves before SADAKO and GRANDMOTHER, using the mylar streamers to suggest fires on the ground before them. SADAKO points to streamers.)* Look, Grandmother!

236 GRANDMOTHER. The Yaizu River.

237 SADAKO. But it's burning.

238 GRANDMOTHER. It is All Soul's Day. The day of the spirits.

239 SADAKO. There are hundreds of little boats with candles!

240 GRANDMOTHER. The spirits have visited their loved ones tonight, just as I have visited you. The candles in the river are "farewell fires." Soon the spirits will join us.

---

5. **mylar streamers** flaps of polyester fabric sometimes used in theatre productions

241 SADAKO. Join *us?* You mean I'll be able to meet the spirits?

242 GRANDMOTHER. Yes.

243 SADAKO. How wonderful! *(She is very excited, anxiously looking down for a glimpse of the SPIRITS. Pointing.)* There! There! Grandmother, look! *(ACTOR 1 moves around them in a circle holding red masks on poles which seem to "float" around SADAKO and GRANDMOTHER.*

244 GRANDMOTHER. Those are spirits of a thousand, thousand years.

245 SADAKO *(delighted).* A thousand, thousand years?

246 GRANDMOTHER. Yes. They were once young like you, Sadako.

247 SADAKO. Like me?

248 GRANDMOTHER. Yes.

249 SADAKO *(pointing).* Look! He looks like an *Emperor! (ACTOR 1 circles around them, holding a parasol above his head. He moves regally and spins at the sound of gongs, which announce his presence. As he moves away, GRANDMOTHER bows to him.)*

250 GRANDMOTHER. Their valley is deep and their mountains hard to climb. We need not visit there. Our mountain is just ahead.

251 ACTOR 1 *(using streamers as wings again).* Five hundred and ninety-three! Five hundred and ninety-four! Five hundred and ninety-five!

252 GRANDMOTHER *(gesturing to a place before them).* Here is where we will stop.

253 *(ACTOR 1 slows the wings; they mime landing with a whoosh sound as before. ACTOR 1 gently flutters the streamers down to a halt. The music changes from excitement to a quiet, eerie sound of wind instruments. This music will continue through the speeches of the SPIRITS. GRANDMOTHER dismounts the crane, gestures to SADAKO to do the same. SADAKO jumps off the crane, excited with anticipation. ACTOR 1 moves bench. GRANDMOTHER offers SADAKO her arm and leads her around the stage. SADAKO is looking eagerly around. ACTOR 1 puts red mask in holder. He stands behind the waist-high mask among the pastel fans.)*

254 GRANDMOTHER *(gesturing toward mask).* This is the spirit of Mr. Araki. *(ACTOR 1 opens an oriental paper parasol. When he speaks for a SPIRIT he*

will stand behind that mask with the parasol opened above his head. He does not alter his voice to suggest SPIRITs' voices.)

255 ACTOR 1/MR. ARAKI. I was helping to build fire lanes for Hiroshima. The enemy may come soon they said, we must build fire lanes. I was digging with my shovel. I saw the metal grow bright before me. I watched it melt. Everything turned white. Then I was here.

256 *(ACTOR 1 moves parasol in front of his face, closes it as he turns away, leaving the red masks. GRANDMOTHER again offers SADAKO her arm and walks her around the stage as ACTOR 1 places another red mask in its holder. SADAKO is growing confused and a little frightened.)*

257 GRANDMOTHER *(gesturing)*. This is the spirit of Mrs. Watanabe.

258 ACTOR 1/MRS. WATANABE *(opens parasol)*. I had just prepared a breakfast for my baby boy. I was bending over his basket to pick him up when I felt a tremendous wind blow me across the room. My baby boy has not joined me here. *(Closes parasol as before, leaving the red mask. Again GRANDMOTHER leads SADAKO on her arm, around and up to third red mask.)*

259 GRANDMOTHER *(gesturing)*. This is the spirit of Daisuke.

260 ACTOR 1/DAISUKE. I was seven years old when I came here. I had studied my lessons hard for an examination. I was walking to school. I looked up to see a bird fly. Suddenly the sky was on fire. *(Closes parasol, moves to music stand, leaving three red masks placed among the pastel fans.)*

261 SADAKO *(horrified, looking at the masks)*. The bomb. They're all talking about the bomb that fell when I was two years old.

262 GRANDMOTHER. The bomb brought me here, Sadako. *(ACTOR 1 begins to count, continues during this conversation.)*

263 ACTOR 1. Six hundred and twenty-eight, six hundred and twenty-nine . . .

264 SADAKO. Yes, I remember.

265 ACTOR 1. Six hundred and thirty-one, six hundred and thirty-two . . .

266 GRANDMOTHER. The bomb has brought you here, Sadako. You must stay with us.

267 SADAKO *(realizing what GRANDMOTHER means, pleading)*. But how can that be? I'm twelve years old now. It's been ten years since the bomb fell.

268 GRANDMOTHER. The bomb continues to fall, Sadako. It is falling even now. *(GRANDMOTHER gestures to ACTOR 1, who pauses in his counting. He brings his head up slowly to look directly at SADAKO. Pause. He resumes his counting.)*

269 SADAKO *(panicking)*. But my cranes! I've been folding my cranes as fast as I can!

270 ACTOR 1. Six hundred and thirty-nine . . .

271 SADAKO *(pleading)*. I haven't folded a thousand yet!

272 GRANDMOTHER *(assuring)*. You will have a thousand. You'll see. It is better to leave them for others to finish.

273 SADAKO. Someone will finish them for me? But then how can the cranes grant my wish?

274 GRANDMOTHER *(lovingly)*. What did you wish for, Sadako? *(ACTOR 1 stops counting but continues percussion rhythm during the following line.)*

275 SADAKO. To make you live. To make me better. I wished that there will never ever be a bomb like that again. *(Silence. ACTOR 1 moves dramatically from music stand carrying closed parasol before him as if it is something very precious. He ceremoniously gives it to GRANDMOTHER, bows and returns to his place behind the music stand. GRANDMOTHER moves to SADAKO, holds parasol out to her, nods to encourage her. SADAKO takes the parasol, GRANDMOTHER moves away. ACTOR 1 begins rhythm again. They count together.)*

276 ACTOR 1 and GRANDMOTHER. Six hundred and forty-one, six hundred and forty-two, six hundred and forty-three . . .

277 SADAKO *(solemn)*. Six hundred and forty-four. *(There is the sound of the bomb as she opens the parasol above her head, then brings it down in front of her, like a shield, hiding her face. GRANDMOTHER and ACTOR 1 bow their heads. The bomb sound continues as SADAKO moves to take her place in the fans with the other red masks. Lifts parasol.)* I was two years old and my mother held me in her arms. She sang a song to me. It was a quiet summer morning. Inside our small house my grandmother was preparing tea. Suddenly there was a tremendous flash of light that cut across the sky. *(She moves her parasol to cover her face as before.)*

NOTES

278 *(The bomb sound is quieter this time and slowly fades away. ACTOR 1 becomes KENJI. KENJI enters the scene calling to SADAKO. He uses the bill of his hat as before to make a large mouth for his comical frog. The bill covers his eyes.)*

279 KENJI *(playful)*. Sadako! Oh, Sadako . . . How's the lazy little turtle this morning? You know, I think you're right. I'm becoming more of a frog every day. Why, just this morning I found two warts on my foot. Now what do you make of that? Croak! See, there's that sound again. *(Hopping to her bed.)* You want to see my warts? *(He puts his cap back to see her, laughing. He is stopped when he sees that she is not there.)* Sadako? *(Looks around.)* Sadako? *(He sees rope of cranes, holds it, then sits on the bench. He solemnly removes his hat and bows his head.)*

280 *(From her place at the music stand, ACTOR 2 narrates.)*

281 ACTOR 2. Sadako Sasaki died on October 25, 1955. Her friends and classmates folded three hundred and fifty-six cranes to make a thousand. *(KENJI stands, moves U, mimes getting the large piece of paper as before. He gracefully places it downstage. The folding music begins, KENJI mimes folding movements of giant crane as SADAKO has done. ACTOR 2 begins recorded folding music and moves from the stand to DL.)* Sadako's friends began to dream of building a monument to her and all the children who were killed by the atom bomb. In 1958, the statue was unveiled in the Hiroshima Peace Park. There is Sadako standing on top of a granite mountain. She is holding a golden crane in outstretched arms.

282 KENJI *(as he folds)*. Nine hundred and ninety-seven . . .

283 ACTOR 2. Now every year, children from all over Japan visit her memorial . . .

284 KENJI. Nine hundred and ninety-eight . . .

285 ACTOR 2. And bring thousands of paper cranes to her monument.

286 KENJI. Nine hundred and ninety-nine . . .

287 ACTOR 2. Their wish is engraved on the base of the statue: *(KENJI begins to stand, slowly miming the lifting of the giant crane. He uses both hands as SADAKO did in the beginning. It is very light.)*

288 "This is our cry,
This is our prayer,
Peace in the World."

Copyright © BookheadEd Learning, LLC

289 KENJI. One thousand. *(He launches it in the air and blows after it as SADAKO has done before. His outstretched arms follow the path of the bird's flight, turning to a point, indicating the flight across the sky. ACTOR 2 watches the bird with KENJI. From her position U, SADAKO moves her parasol from its shield-like position, holding it above her head. She watches the flight of the bird with KENJI and ACTOR 2. She points up.)*

290 SADAKO *(joyous).* Look, Grandmother! You were right! *(ALL freeze.)*

THE END

Please note that excerpts and passages in the StudySync® library and this workbook are intended as touchstones to generate interest in an author's work. The excerpts and passages do not substitute for the reading of entire texts, and StudySync® strongly recommends that students seek out and purchase the whole literary or informational work in order to experience it as the author intended. Links to online resellers are available in our digital library. In addition, complete works may be ordered through an authorized reseller by filling out and returning to StudySync® the order form enclosed in this workbook.

Reading & Writing
Companion

29

First Read

Read *A Thousand Cranes*. After you read, complete the Think Questions below.

☁ THINK QUESTIONS

1. Briefly explain how Sadako felt upon learning the impact of radiation on her physical health despite the fact that she was "only two when the bomb fell." Use evidence from the text to support your explanation.

2. How does the creation of crane origami contribute to the theme of peace? Be specific and be sure to cite evidence from the story.

3. How might *A Thousand Cranes* be described as a biography? Cite textual evidence to support your answer.

4. The word **discipline** comes from the Latin *disciplina*, which means "instruction, knowledge." With that information in mind, write a definition of *discipline* as it is used in this story. How does your definition compare to or contrast with the Latin definition? Explain, and cite context clues that helped you arrive at your understanding of the word.

5. Use context clues to determine the meaning of the word **subdued.** Write your best definition here, along with words or phrases from the text that were helpful in coming to your conclusion. Finally, check a dictionary to confirm your understanding.

Skill:
Character

Use the Checklist to analyze Character in *A Thousand Cranes*. Refer to the sample student annotations about Character in the text.

••• CHECKLIST FOR CHARACTER

In order to determine how particular elements of a story or drama interact, note the following:

✓ the characters in the story, including the protagonist and antagonist

✓ the settings and how they shape the characters or plot

✓ plot events and how they affect the characters

✓ key events or series of episodes in the plot, especially events that cause characters to react, respond, or change in some way

✓ characters' responses as the plot reaches a climax and moves toward a resolution of the problem facing the protagonist

✓ the resolution of the conflict in the plot and the ways that affects each character

To analyze how particular elements of a story or drama interact, consider the following questions:

✓ How do the characters' responses change or develop from the beginning to the end of the story?

✓ How does the setting shape the characters and plot in the story?

✓ How do the events in the plot affect the characters? How do characters develop as a result of the conflict, climax, and resolution?

Please note that excerpts and passages in the StudySync® library and this workbook are intended as touchstones to generate interest in an author's work. The excerpts and passages do not substitute for the reading of entire texts, and StudySync® strongly recommends that students seek out and purchase the whole literary or informational work in order to experience it as the author intended. Links to online resellers are available in our digital library. In addition, complete works may be ordered through an authorized reseller by filling out and returning to StudySync® the order form enclosed in this workbook.

Reading & Writing
Companion

31

Skill:
Character

Reread lines 200–204 of *A Thousand Cranes*. Then, using the Checklist on the previous page, answer the multiple-choice questions below.

↻ YOUR TURN

1. Based on the dialogue and stage directions in lines 200–204, the reader can conclude that —

   ○ A. Sadako is upset and worried about getting better.
   ○ B. Sadako is hopeful that the cranes will help her.
   ○ C. Sadako is bored and tired of being in the hospital.
   ○ D. Her parents are upset by the cranes.

2. This question has two parts. First, answer Part A. Then, answer Part B.

   Part A: What do the dialogue and stage directions in line 204 reveal about Sadako?

   ○ A. that her priorities have changed since she became ill
   ○ B. that she wants only to rest now
   ○ C. that she is still focused on racing when she gets better
   ○ D. that she is frightened of her illness

   Part B: Which of the following details best supports your response to Part A?

   ○ A. "It's kind of like a race anyway, don't you think?"
   ○ B. "Kenji said I was better than the girl who ran."
   ○ C. "Father. I'll make you so proud of me!"
   ○ D. "Folding cranes is much better than any old race."

Skill: Dramatic Elements and Structure

Use the Checklist to analyze Dramatic Elements and Structure in *A Thousand Cranes*. Refer to the sample student annotations about Dramatic Elements and Structure in the text.

••• CHECKLIST FOR DRAMATIC ELEMENTS AND STRUCTURE

In order to identify the dramatic elements and structure of a drama, note the following:

- ✓ the form of the drama, such as comedy or tragedy

- ✓ how the acts and scenes advance the plot

- ✓ the setting of the play and whether or how it changes in each act or scene

- ✓ the language of the play, such as prose or verse, as spoken by characters

- ✓ the use of dramatic devices such as

  - soliloquy or monologue, when a character speaks his or her thoughts aloud directly to the audience while alone on stage

  - asides, when a character shares private thoughts with the audience when other characters are on stage

  - the information in stage directions, including lighting, sound, and set, as well as details about characters, including exits and entrances

To analyze how a drama's form or structure contributes to its meaning, consider the following questions:

- ✓ How does the use of stage directions contribute to the play's meaning or message?

- ✓ How is each act or scene structured? How do characters enter and leave, how do they speak to each other, and what happens as a result?

- ✓ How does the drama's form or structure contribute to the play's meaning or message?

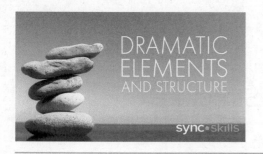

Skill: Dramatic Elements and Structure

Reread lines 270–278 of *A Thousand Cranes*. Then, using the Checklist on the previous page, answer the multiple-choice questions below.

YOUR TURN

1. This question has two parts. First, answer Part A. Then, answer Part B.

   Part A: How do the sound elements in the scene help you identify the form of the play?

   - ○ A. The sound elements make the play feel like a spooky tragedy.
   - ○ B. The sound elements make the play feel like a comedy.
   - ○ C. The sound elements make the play feel like a serious tragedy.
   - ○ D. The sound elements do not help the reader identify the form of the play.

   Part B: Which of the following details BEST supports your response to Part A?

   - ○ A. GRANDMOTHER *(lovingly).* What did you wish for, Sadako? *(ACTOR 1 stops counting)*
   - ○ B. SADAKO. To make you live. To make me better. I wished that there will never ever be a bomb like that again. *(Silence. ACTOR 1 moves dramatically from music stand)*
   - ○ C. *She opens the parasol above her head, then brings it down in front of her, like a shield, hiding her face. GRANDMOTHER and ACTOR 1 bow their heads.*
   - ○ D. I was two years old and my mother held me in her arms. She sang a song to me. It was a quiet summer morning.

Close Read

Reread *A Thousand Cranes*. As you reread, complete the Skills Focus questions below. Then use your answers and annotations from the questions to help you complete the Write activity.

◎ SKILLS FOCUS

1. Sadako is a happy and hopeful child. Identify dialogue and/or stage directions that show this, and explain how her qualities affect the other people in the neighborhood.

2. The sound elements of the play contribute to its tone. Identify evidence of the sound elements adding to the tone of the play and explain the effect of the sound elements.

3. The drama *A Thousand Cranes* is a tragedy. It also offers a hopeful and positive message. Identify evidence that supports the play's message or deeper meaning. Explain what society can learn from Sadako's story.

4. Sadako and Jonah in *The Giver* both have complicated relationships with their futures. Compare how the characters are developed in the two stories.

5. *The Giver*, *Nothing to Envy*, and *A Thousand Cranes* all involve characters that stand out in very different ways. Identify how Sadako stands out from the crowd in *A Thousand Cranes* and explain what causes her to stand out.

✎ WRITE

DISCUSSION: *The Giver, Nothing to Envy,* and *A Thousand Cranes* all feature children reacting to their societies. What do these three texts suggest about the relationship between the individual and society? To prepare for your discussion, use the graphic organizer to write down your ideas about the prompt. Support your ideas with evidence from the text. After your discussion, write a reflection.

Remarks
at the UNESCO
Education for
All Week Luncheon

INFORMATIONAL TEXT
Laura Bush
2006

Introduction

S oon after her husband George W. Bush was elected president in 2000, Laura Bush (b. 1946) promised to make education a major focus during her time as first lady. In 2006, Mrs. Bush was named an honorary ambassador for the United Nations' Decade of Literacy. Shortly after that, she gave this speech, announcing that she would host the first-ever White House Conference on Global Literacy. The announcement was made at an event celebrating Education for All Week, a multinational event put on by the United Nations Educational, Scientific and Cultural Organization (UNESCO). Mrs. Bush's work in education began as a teacher and a librarian. In this speech, she draws on her experiences as an educator in order to promote the conference's theme of "Every Child Needs a Teacher."

"Literacy and freedom are inseparable."

NOTES

1   Thank you, Secretary Spellings, for the very kind introduction, and for the great work that you're doing for young people.

2   I also want to thank Ambassador[1] Ensenat and the State Department for hosting this event. Learning — whether it's about other cultures and countries, or about ourselves — is at the heart of diplomacy. So I appreciate your bringing us together today to discuss how we can better educate the world's children.

First Lady Laura Bush delivers remarks at an Education for All Luncheon in Washington, D.C.

3   I'd also like to acknowledge UNESCO's Assistant Director General for Education, Peter Smith. Peter, thank you so much for joining us today. And, of course, I want to thank all of Your Excellencies, the very distinguished ambassadors who are here with us. We're joined today by all of the female ambassadors here in Washington, and I knew there was a reason Ambassador Ensenat was looking so sharp. (Laughter.) So thank you, ambassadors. Thank you for coming, and for your commitment to education.

4   We're also joined by a number of people that I've known since my husband was governor, as we've worked on reading issues, first in Texas and then in the United States. Some **experts** in literacy are here with you today. I think maybe everyone has at least one expert on literacy at their table, so I hope you'll get to know them and talk to them.

5   As the Honorary Ambassador of the United Nations Literacy Decade, I'm happy to be with you to mark the beginning of Education for All Week, and to talk about why Every Child Needs a Teacher.

Skill: Reasons and Evidence

The ideas of "Education for All" and "Every Child Needs a Teacher" imply that more teachers are needed because every child deserves a formal education.

---

1. **ambassador** a diplomat acting as an official representative of a country in international relations

Skill: Reasons
and Evidence

This paragraph offers a reason to support the claim that more teachers are needed. The reason is that many children around the world are growing up without teachers and without a formal education. Two pieces of evidence support this reason: 100 million children do not have access to school (numerical data), and HIV/AIDS is devastating the teaching population in Africa (a fact).

6   All of us can remember the teachers who made a difference in our lives. Margaret just told us about her Ms. Brown. My favorite was my second grade teacher, Ms. Gnagy. I wanted to grow up and be just like her. And I did, so I became a teacher, and then a librarian. And I was with her last week in Midland, Texas, when I was out there when the George Bush childhood home was dedicated, the home that President George Bush Number 41, as we call him, and President Bush Number 43 and Governor Jeb Bush from Florida all lived in in the 1950s. It was a house the Bushes bought in 1951. And while I was there, my second grade teacher, Ms. Gnagy, was there at the luncheon, and George's second grade teacher, Ms. Watson, was there, as well. (Laughter.) So that's so fun to have this long history with teachers that meant so much to us.

7   I know that who we are today, all of us, every one of us in this room, who we are is because of teachers that we had throughout our lives. Many children across the globe, though, are growing up without teachers and without any hope for a formal education. Around the world, more than 100 million children do not have access to schools. The situation is especially serious in Africa, where HIV/AIDS is devastating the teaching population.

8   Training more teachers is vital to UNESCO's goal of making sure every child has access to a basic, quality education by 2015. This is important for every country, but especially for developing countries[2], where limited resources often mean that the neediest children are not educated. We have to make sure that all children — boys and girls, rich and poor — have access to a good education.

9   One of the best ways we can improve educational opportunities for all is by spreading literacy. And one of the most important reasons every child should have a teacher is so that every child can learn to read.

10 There's no such thing as a quality, basic education for a person who cannot read or write. Reading is the bedrock on which the entire mind is built — one book, one essay, one instruction manual at a time. And reading doesn't just allow people to enjoy literary treasures. It allows them to become entrepreneurs[3], or engineers, or lawmakers, or doctors. In villages around the world, mothers who read can then teach their children how to read. Literate mothers can also participate in their economies, and they can earn a living for themselves and their families. So widespread literacy isn't a luxury for healthy societies — it's a basic requirement.

---

2. **developing countries** typically referring to poorer and/or more agrarian nations that are not caught up to Western standards of industrialization or wealth
3. **entrepreneur** a successful business person who organizes and manages a business

NOTES

11 Across the globe, more than 800 million people are **illiterate**. Eighty-five percent of them live in just 34 countries, concentrated in regions affected by poverty. And more than two-thirds of the 771 million adults who cannot read a simple book, or write a basic sentence, are women.

12 I've visited many countries around the world, and I've seen how efforts to expand literacy are improving lives, especially for women and girls.

13 Last year, I visited the Women's Teacher Training Institute in Kabul, which was established through a partnership between the government of Afghanistan and USAID. At the Institute, which is also a dorm so that women who come in from the provinces to study have a safe place to live, women are then trained to be teachers. Then they go home and they train more teachers in a cascading effect with an attempt to train about 6,000 teachers in a very short amount of time so that the schools in Afghanistan, as they're being rebuilt, will have teachers.

14 In January, I was in Ghana, at the Accra Teacher Training College. Ghana is participating in the Textbooks and Learning Materials Program. As part of the program, six American universities, minority-serving universities, have partnered with six African countries to produce and **distribute** 15 million primary school textbooks — that would be kindergarten through eighth grade textbooks — for African students. The Textbook program is part of President Bush's African Education Initiative, a $600 million commitment that's already helped to train more than 300,000 teachers in sub-Saharan Africa.

15 And these textbooks, in the Textbook program, will be published in Africa. They'll be written with the help of these U.S. universities, with African educators, so that the books are Africa-centric, they're traditional, they talk about things that children who are studying them know about and live with every day.

16 Then, last month in Pakistan, I met with teachers and students involved in UNESCO and Children Resources International programs that improve teacher training and **promote** family literacy. I talked with Mehnaz Aziz, the Pakistan country director for Children's Resources International. Mehnaz shared with me how over the last three years, CRI has been training teachers in new methodologies. Before, teachers lacked instructional materials, and they used rote memorization and corporal punishment. Now they have money for school buildings, teaching aids and materials, and children can learn through drama and art.

17 Mehnaz also told me that before, parents had little involvement with their children's schools. But now mothers were coming, Mehnaz said. "It's one of the big changes. Reading — the mothers are also learning, reading books, and reading with their children."

Copyright © BookheadEd Learning, LLC

18   Teaching people to read and write is about more than just improving literacy skills. Another Pakistani educator, Fakhira Najib, said to me, "The students aren't just learning reading and writing. They're curious now." These are just some of the examples of the difference a commitment to education and literacy is making worldwide. These strides come at such an important time, as we witness a tide of freedom spreading across the globe. This is not a coincidence. Literacy and freedom are inseparable.

19   Literacy is the foundation of personal freedom. Being able to read, and choosing what we read, is how we shape our beliefs, our minds, and our characters. Reading brings self-reliance and independence. For many women and their children, literacy can even mean the difference between life and death. A mother who can read can understand the label on a food container. She knows how to follow the instructions on a bottle of medicine. She's more likely to make wise decisions about her life that will keep her and her children healthy.

20   Literacy is the foundation of economic freedom. Free markets require informed consumers, and that means consumers who can read. Wider literacy also increases economic participation, which leads to more stable and vibrant economies. When we launched the U.N. Literacy Decade in New York, we were joined by a woman from the Philippines, Pampay Usman. Growing up, Pampay didn't have the opportunity to go to school. And although she couldn't read or write, she was able to manage a small market. You can imagine how hard and frustrating her work was, because she couldn't write down the names of her customers, or the goods they bought. She had to remember their faces, and every item they purchased.

21   The day Pampay joined an adult literacy class in her village, her life changed forever. She learned to write her name and address. She learned to read prices on groceries, and her business grew. Pampay is an example of how teaching one woman to read can lead to greater prosperity for herself and for the others who depend upon her.

22   Literacy is also the basis of political freedom. Around the world, more and more countries are embracing democracy and liberty. But for people to participate in a democracy, they have to be educated about their country's laws and traditions, which means they have to be able to read.

23   We saw this last October, when millions of copies of Iraq's draft constitution were printed and distributed to voters. Millions of Iraqis read their proposed charter, and then braved the threat of violence to cast their ballots. They risked their lives for a written document, language that enshrines their rights, and charts their future course for their new democracy.

24   Literacy improves the lives of mothers and children. Literacy boosts economies. And literacy helps people make good, informed decisions about their health.

25   Today, I'm delighted to announce that this September, during the opening of the 61st session of the U.N. General Assembly, we'll convene a Conference on Global Literacy in New York. Working in cooperation with the U.S. Department of Education, the U.S. State Department, the U.S. Agency for International Development, and UNESCO, the United Nations Scientific and Cultural Organization, we'll be looking at literacy programs that work, and connecting countries with the information they need to implement similar programs. The Conference will also encourage leaders from around the world to become involved in literacy in their own countries, and then to learn ways to support UNESCO's goal of Education for All by 2015.

26   This week, as we work to make sure that Every Child Has a Teacher, it's important to remember that we're all teachers. A person who's never stood by a blackboard still teaches by example. By **demonstrating** our commitment to literacy, we can let millions of people know that reading and writing are important.

27   So thank you for having me here today. Thank you for your commitment to education. And I hope I'll see you at the Conference in New York in September. Thank you all very much.

REMARKS AT THE **UNESCO EDUCATION FOR ALL WEEK** LUNCHEON

First Read

Read "Remarks at the UNESCO Education for All Week Luncheon." After you read, complete the Think Questions below.

☁ THINK QUESTIONS

1. What skill does Bush see as the foundation of a good education? Cite places in the text where she emphasizes this important skill.

2. What specific types of freedom does Bush say will be promoted by the spread of literacy? Refer to paragraphs 19–22 in your response.

3. Name two nations where Bush is attempting to promote literacy goals. Provide evidence from the text of ways the literacy initiatives she mentions will have a direct impact in these countries.

4. Use context clues to determine the meaning of **illiterate** as it is used in paragraph 11 of "Remarks at the UNESCO Education for All Week Luncheon." Write your definition here and identify clues that helped you figure out its meaning.

5. Keeping in mind that the Latin prefix *dis-* means "apart" and the root *tribuere* means "to give," write your definition of **distribute** here.

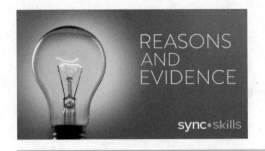

Skill:
Reasons and Evidence

Use the Checklist to analyze Reasons and Evidence in "Remarks at the UNESCO Education for All Week Luncheon." Refer to the sample student annotations about Reasons and Evidence in the text.

••• CHECKLIST FOR REASONS AND EVIDENCE

In order to identify the reasons and evidence that support the speaker's claim(s) in an argument, note the following:

- ✓ the argument the speaker is making

- ✓ the claim or the main idea of the argument

- ✓ the reasons and evidence that support the claim and where they can be found

- ✓ if the evidence the author presents to support the claim is sound, or complete and comprehensive

- ✓ if there is sufficient evidence to support the claim or if more is needed

To assess whether the speaker's reasoning is sound and the evidence is relevant and sufficient, consider the following questions:

- ✓ What kind of argument is the speaker making?

- ✓ Is the reasoning, or the thinking behind the claims, sound and valid?

- ✓ Are the reasons and evidence the speaker presents to support the claim sufficient, or is more evidence needed? Why or why not?

Please note that excerpts and passages in the StudySync® library and this workbook are intended as touchstones to generate interest in an author's work. The excerpts and passages do not substitute for the reading of entire texts, and StudySync® strongly recommends that students seek out and purchase the whole literary or informational work in order to experience it as the author intended. Links to online resellers are available in our digital library. In addition, complete works may be ordered through an authorized reseller by filling out and returning to StudySync® the order form enclosed in this workbook.

Reading & Writing
Companion

43

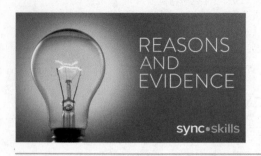

Skill:
Reasons and Evidence

Reread paragraphs 20–22 from "Remarks at the UNESCO Education for All Week Luncheon." Then, using the Checklist on the previous page, answer the multiple-choice questions below.

YOUR TURN

1. Mrs. Bush uses the personal story of Pampay Usman as —

    ○ A. the claim, or central idea, of her argument.

    ○ B. a piece of evidence that supports economic freedom as a reason why learning to read is important.

    ○ C. a piece of evidence that supports political freedom as a reason why learning to read is important.

    ○ D. a reason for drawing attention to illiteracy among women.

2. Which general statement does Mrs. Bush imply by the reasons and evidence she presents in her speech?

    ○ A. People who live in democracies should be required by law to learn to read.

    ○ B. People have to learn to read before they will demand democratic governments.

    ○ C. Teaching adults to read and write is just as important as teaching children.

    ○ D. Many women have children and others who are economically dependent on them.

REMARKS AT THE **UNESCO EDUCATION FOR ALL WEEK** LUNCHEON

Close Read

Reread "Remarks at the UNESCO Education for All Week Luncheon." As you reread, complete the Skills Focus questions below. Then use your answers and annotations from the questions to help you complete the Write activity.

◎ SKILLS FOCUS

1. Identify various types of evidence that Mrs. Bush uses. Explain how that evidence helps to support her argument.

2. Mrs. Bush is speaking to a very specific audience in this speech. Identify language that helps create the tone of the speech, and write a note about how that tone is appropriate for the audience.

3. Identify where Bush states a main or central idea in the speech and write a note about how she develops that idea in the following paragraphs.

4. Identify parts of Laura Bush's speech that describe the effects of education on individuals. Explain how personal achievements, especially learning how to read and write, can help a person stand out from the crowd.

✏ WRITE

ARGUMENTATIVE: In "Remarks at the UNESCO Education for All Week Luncheon," Laura Bush argues that literacy is vital for all children. What are Mrs. Bush's main claims? How does she use reasons and evidence to support her argument and claims sufficiently? Be sure to use evidence from the text in your response.

Please note that excerpts and passages in the StudySync® library and this workbook are intended as touchstones to generate interest in an author's work. The excerpts and passages do not substitute for the reading of entire texts, and StudySync® strongly recommends that students seek out and purchase the whole literary or informational work in order to experience it as the author intended. Links to online resellers are available in our digital library. In addition, complete works may be ordered through an authorized reseller by filling out and returning to StudySync® the order form enclosed in this workbook.

Reading & Writing Companion   45

Hidden Figures

INFORMATIONAL TEXT
Margot Lee Shetterly
2016

Introduction

argot Lee Shetterly's *Hidden Figures* is the story of African American women in the 1940s and '50s who overcame great obstacles in their careers as aeronautical engineers. These women, called "computers" because they calculated numbers, persevered at a time in history when not only were most professions closed to women, but also when racial discrimination was legal. In 2016, their story was brought to the screen with Taraji P. Henson, Octavia Spencer, and Janelle Monáe.

"There was only one way to find out: try it."

from Chapter 9

Specialization

1   Men often came to the laboratory as junior engineers and were allowed to design and conduct their own experiments. Researchers took the men under their wings, teaching them the ropes. Women, on the other hand, had to work much harder to overcome other people's low expectations. A woman who worked in the central computing pool was one step removed from the research, and the engineers' assignments sometimes lacked the context to give the computer much knowledge about the project.

2   The work of most of the women was anonymous. Even a woman who had worked closely with an engineer on a research report rarely saw her name on the final **publication**. The engineers assumed it didn't matter; after all, she was just a woman, and many of the men were blind to the fact that a woman might have the same **ambitions** as a man.

3   Sometimes a computer's work impressed an engineer so much that he invited her to join him working full-time with a wind tunnel group[1]. For the women, this meant an opportunity to get closer to the research, and perhaps specialize in a particular subfield of aeronautics[2]. A computer who could not only process data but also understand how to **interpret** it was more valuable to the team than a pool computer with more general knowledge. Specialization became the key to managing the increasingly complex nature of aeronautical research in the postwar era.

Sonic Boom

4   Many of the Langley engineers shared a dream: they wanted to design an aircraft capable of flying faster than the speed of sound. And the women at

NOTES

 Skill: Author's Purpose and Point of View

Shetterly describes how male junior engineers worked versus female employees. These details show that the author's purpose is to inform readers that women had a harder time being directly involved in research. The author's language makes me think she views this treatment as unfair.

---

1. **wind tunnel group** a group of researchers at NASA who design and test new generations of aircraft, both commercial and military, as well as NASA space vehicles, including the Space Shuttle
2. **aeronautics** the theory and practice of navigation through air

Please note that excerpts and passages in the StudySync® library and this workbook are intended as touchstones to generate interest in an author's work. The excerpts and passages do not substitute for the reading of entire texts, and StudySync® strongly recommends that students seek out and purchase the whole literary or informational work in order to experience it as the author intended. Links to online resellers are available in our digital library. In addition, complete works may be ordered through an authorized reseller by filling out and returning to StudySync® the order form enclosed in this workbook.

Reading & Writing Companion   47

Skill: Technical Language

I have not heard the phrase sonic boom before. This essay is about aeronautical engineering. The author used the term sonic boom to describe how they pierced the sound barrier, so sonic boom might mean "a big sound."

Skill: Author's Purpose and Point of View

The author gives more facts and details about the female computers' role for this project. The author's purpose is to inform about their contributions and importance to the success of NASA's projects. We learn that they worked hard to contribute to the success of research and were promoted for their efforts.

Langley were no exception. They dreamed of this exciting possibility, which was seeming less far-fetched by the day. To pursue this dream, in 1947, a group of thirteen employees, including two former East Computers, were sent to the Mojave Desert in the western part of the United States to establish a high-speed flight research center. Their mission: to build the fastest airplane in the world, one that could fly faster than the speed of sound.

5   The speed of sound is about 760 miles per hour. The exact number varies, depending on temperature, altitude, and humidity. Scientists used to think that flying faster than the speed of sound was impossible! But they were wrong.

6   "Mach 1" is the term for something moving at the speed of sound. When an object is moving this fast, the air molecules in front of the object can't get out of the way quickly enough, so they become compressed and form a shock wave. That shock wave is the noise we hear from the crack of a bullwhip or the firing of a bullet.

7   Scientists weren't sure what would happen to a pilot or his plane if he flew at Mach 1. Some researchers thought that the plane or the pilot would be destroyed by the power of the shock wave. Others disagreed.

8   There was only one way to find out: try it.

9   On October 14, 1947, pilot Chuck Yeager flew over the Mojave Desert in an NACA-developed experimental research plane called the Bell X-1. And he pierced the sound barrier for the first time in history! The plane caused a loud noise—a sonic boom, just like the shockwave from the bullet and the bullwhip—but the pilot and the plane were safe. The female computers on the ground verified the data **transmitted** from the instruments attached to the X-1 on its record-breaking flight.

10 At the Mojave Desert facility, the computers who helped with this experiment had the chance to do significant work and get credit for it. They were promoted from "computer" to the higher position of "junior engineer," and were named as the authors of research reports, a necessary first step in the career of an engineer. And for a woman, it was an extraordinary achievement. It meant that the whole world would see that she had contributed to a worthy piece of research, and that she was an important member of an engineering team.

11 Dorothy Hoover, another black woman who worked in West Computing, was the first African-American woman to leave the computing pool and get a chance at a research job, working directly for an engineer. She had earned an undergraduate degree in math from Arkansas Agricultural, Mechanical & Normal College and a master's degree in mathematics from Atlanta University, and she taught in three states before coming to Langley in 1943. She was excellent at **abstract** concepts and complex equations. She had been assigned many of the most challenging problems and always submitted flawless work.

NOTES

12 As a talented mathematician with an independent mind, Dorothy Hoover was a perfect addition to any research team. Her visibility with engineers increased with her promotion. She answered the computers' questions and understood complex math so well that she sometimes knew more than many of the engineers in the lab.

The Section Leader

13 Dorothy Vaughan was an excellent leader within the West Area computing pool. In 1947, one of her bosses got sick and was out of the office for a month. The next year, the boss fell ill again. Then, in early 1949, Dorothy's boss began to act strangely at work. She suffered a mental breakdown and was forced to leave her job.

14 This tragic incident left the computing pool without a leader. But the engineers at the laboratory decided to choose Dorothy to be the temporary head of the entire section. This was the first time an African-American woman had been assigned a management role at Langley. At the time, it was unthinkable for a man to report to a woman. Men were always ultimately the people in charge. Women who had an interest in management were limited to heading a section in one of the computing pools or a division with female workers—but they always reported to a man. For Dorothy, the new job was a lot like being at the head of a high school classroom and reporting to a principal, who was usually a man.

15 It would take Dorothy Vaughan two years to earn the full title of "section head." The men she worked for held her in limbo[3]: the laboratory had never had a black supervisor before, and they may have delayed making what seemed like a groundbreaking decision. Dorothy, however, was patient. Her promotion was made official when a memo circulated in January 1951: "Effective this date, Dorothy J. Vaughan, who has been acting head of West Area Computers unit, is hereby appointed head of that unit."

16 Dorothy took on the new responsibilities with confidence. Many of the women in West Computing knew she was the best candidate, and so did many engineers. In time her bosses realized it, too. History would prove them all right: there was no one better qualified for the job than Dorothy Vaughan.

Excerpted from *Hidden Figures* by Margot Lee Shetterly, published by HarperCollins.

---

3. **limbo** a period of waiting for a decision that is uncertain

Skill: Technical Language

Laboratory is a technical term. The context tells me it is the place where Dorothy Vaughan worked. Before this paragraph, we know she was in a different building from the engineers. Using the word *laboratory* here shows the importance of Dorothy Vaughan's promotion and her contributions to science and math.

First Read

Read *Hidden Figures*. After you read, complete the Think Questions below.

Copyright © BookheadEd Learning, LLC

☁ THINK QUESTIONS

1. Why did the engineers working on the project to break the sound barrier have to analyze data from instruments attached to the X-1 aircraft?

2. What kind of educational background did Dorothy Hoover have? Why was that background appropriate for her job?

3. Why did it take Dorothy Vaughan longer than it might have for other engineers to become head of her unit?

4. Use context clues to determine the meaning of **transmit** as it is used in paragraph 9 of *Hidden Figures*. Write your definition here and identify clues that helped you figure out its meaning.

5. Read the following dictionary entry:

   interpret in·ter·pret \in 'tər prət\ *verb*

   1. to translate orally or in sign language the words of a person speaking another language
   2. to explain the meaning of (information, words, or actions)
   3. to reenact in a particular way that conveys one's understanding of a creator's ideas

   Which definition most closely matches the meaning of **interpret** as it is used in paragraph 3? Write the correct definition of *interpret* here and explain how you figured out the correct meaning.

Skill:
Technical Language

Use the Checklist to analyze Technical Language in *Hidden Figures*. Refer to the sample student annotations about Technical Language in the text.

In order to determine the meanings of words and phrases as they are used in a text, note the following:

- ✓ the subject of the book or article

- ✓ any unfamiliar words that you think might be technical terms

- ✓ words that have multiple meanings that change when used with a specific subject

- ✓ the possible contextual meaning of a word, or the definition from a dictionary

To determine the meanings of words and phrases as they are used in a text, including technical meanings, consider the following questions:

- ✓ What is the subject of the informational text?

- ✓ How does the use of technical language help establish the author as an authority on the subject?

- ✓ Are there any technical words that have an impact on the meaning and tone, or quality, of the book or article?

- ✓ Can you identify the contextual meaning of any of the words?

Please note that excerpts and passages in the StudySync® library and this workbook are intended as touchstones to generate interest in an author's work. The excerpts and passages do not substitute for the reading of entire texts, and StudySync® strongly recommends that students seek out and purchase the whole literary or informational work in order to experience it as the author intended. Links to online resellers are available in our digital library. In addition, complete works may be ordered through an authorized reseller by filling out and returning to StudySync® the order form enclosed in this workbook.

Reading & Writing
Companion

51

Skill:
Technical Language

Reread paragraphs 4–5 of *Hidden Figures*. Then, using the Checklist on the previous page, answer the multiple-choice questions below.

↻ YOUR TURN

1. This question has two parts. First, answer Part A. Then, answer Part B.

   Part A: Which sentence below contains multiple technical terms specific to space exploration?

   ○ A. Their mission: to build the fastest airplane in the world, one that could fly faster than the speed of sound.

   ○ B. The speed of sound is about 760 miles per hour.

   ○ C. The exact number varies, depending on temperature, altitude, and humidity.

   ○ D. Scientists used to think that flying faster than the speed of sound was impossible!

   Part B: What is the effect of the technical terms in Part A?

   ○ A. The technical language used makes the paragraph easier to read.

   ○ B. The technical language used communicates the complexity of the work the women supported.

   ○ C. The technical language used establishes the author as an authority on the subject.

   ○ D. The technical language used helps the author explain why human computers were important.

Skill: Author's Purpose and Point of View

Use the Checklist to analyze Author's Purpose and Point of View in *Hidden Figures*. Refer to the sample student annotations about Author's Purpose and Point of View in the text.

••• CHECKLIST FOR AUTHOR'S PURPOSE AND POINT OF VIEW

In order to identify author's purpose and point of view, note the following:

✓ facts, statistics, and graphic aids, as these indicate that the author is writing to inform.

✓ descriptive or sensory details and emotional language may indicate that the author is writing to describe and dramatize events.

✓ descriptions that present a complicated process in plain language may indicate that the author is writing to explain.

✓ emotional language with a call to action may indicate that the author is trying to persuade readers or stress an opinion.

✓ the language the author uses can also be clues to the author's point of view on a subject or topic.

To determine the author's purpose and point of view in a text, consider the following questions:

✓ How does the author convey, or communicate, information in the text?

✓ Does the author use figurative or emotional language? How does it affect the purpose and point of view?

Please note that excerpts and passages in the StudySync® library and this workbook are intended as touchstones to generate interest in an author's work. The excerpts and passages do not substitute for the reading of entire texts, and StudySync® strongly recommends that students seek out and purchase the whole literary or informational work in order to experience it as the author intended. Links to online resellers are available in our digital library. In addition, complete works may be ordered through an authorized reseller by filling out and returning to StudySync® the order form enclosed in this workbook.

Reading & Writing
Companion

53

Skill: Author's Purpose and Point of View

Reread paragraphs 4–8 of *Hidden Figures*. Then, using the Checklist on the previous page, answer the multiple-choice questions below.

↻ YOUR TURN

1. Based on the details in paragraph 4, the reader can conclude that —

   ○ A. the author wants to persuade readers to become aeronautical engineers.

   ○ B. the author wants to inform readers that both men and women shared a dream to build a plane faster than sound.

   ○ C. the author wants to entertain readers with a far-fetched story.

   ○ D. the author wants to inform readers about the role of men in research.

2. The discussion of Mach 1 in paragraphs 6–8 reveals the author's point of view that —

   ○ A. temperature, altitude, and humidity affect the speed of sound.

   ○ B. scientists were foolish to test the boundaries of engineering knowledge.

   ○ C. flying at Mach 1 was an important milestone in engineering research.

   ○ D. Mach 1 is the most dangerous speed to fly an airplane.

Close Read

Reread *Hidden Figures*. As you reread, complete the Skills Focus questions below. Then use your answers and annotations from the questions to help you complete the Write activity.

◎ SKILLS FOCUS

1. Identify details about the author's purpose and point of view in the "Specialization" section of the text. Explain how these details reveal what the author is trying to express.

2. Identify the point of view in "The Section Leader," starting at paragraph 13. Explain why the author may have used this point of view to explain these events.

3. In *Hidden Figures,* the African-American women featured in the text had to overcome many challenges before they were able to engage actively in research with their male colleagues. Using textual evidence, identify an instance of discrimination in *Hidden Figures.*

4. Identify two or three technical terms in the excerpt. Define these words using context clues or a dictionary. Then explain how each word impacts the meaning or tone of the text.

5. The author of *Hidden Figures* tells how Dorothy Vaughan rose to position of "section head"—the first for an African-American woman—and was eventually held in high esteem by her colleagues in the computer pool and the research department. Explain how personal achievements, like these, help a person stand out from the crowd.

✏ WRITE

LITERARY ANALYSIS: What is the author's purpose and point of view in the excerpt from *Hidden Figures*? How does the author's use of technical words impact the excerpt's meaning or tone? Write a response answering these questions using specific examples from the text.

Miami Dancer Follows Dreams While Planning for the Future

INFORMATIONAL TEXT
Mekeisha Madden Toby
2018

Introduction

Journalist and cultural critic Mekeisha Madden Toby profiles Elijah Omary Muhammad, one of the finalists for the prestigious National YoungArts Foundation competition. Muhammad was chosen from a pool of over ten thousand applicants from the visual, literary, design and performing arts disciplines. In this profile, Muhammad outlines his work ethic, his inspiration, and his goals for

"There's a bridge that connects everything and I've found that bridge."

1   The wave of rhythm that slowly takes over eighteen-year-old dancer Elijah Omary Muhammad's body begins as a motion in his right arm, extending to his left arm and then his left leg before he takes a few steps and turns around.

2   This is the intro to the dance routine that helped make Elijah one of the National YoungArts Foundation's 170 finalists from ten different artistic **disciplines**. An estimated 10,000 young performers applied, but Elijah's dedication and **panache** make him unique.

A Different Approach

3   "I do this a little bit differently than most people," says Elijah, who goes by the stage name "IntEnsE" and works tirelessly to live up to his nickname. "When I went to YoungArts, everybody had their own way and style of choreography[1], but I did mine in my living room."

4   "Sometimes, I would put earphones in and just focus on the intricate beats," he says. "I would do the moves over and over again until I could mentally see myself doing it. I used my instincts to figure out what should come next when I looked in the mirror. It's a very strong song so I felt it."

5   The song Elijah chose is called "Mercy" by Jacob Banks, a tune that first gained attention during a tragic scene on the premium cable drama "Power"— but when the Miami Northwestern Senior High School graduate arranged his hip-hop-inspired dance moves using this music, the effect was more dramatic than **melancholy**.

6   Although the routine itself is very serious, Elijah's playful nature shines through via his facial expressions and poked-out tongue. "I learned everything I know watching cartoons," Elijah says. "When I was younger, I'd watch 'Tom and Jerry' and 'Looney Tunes' and watch how they'd move. I would rewind and

---

1. **choreography** the specific steps and movements that are associated with a dance or other organized movement

Skill: Media

The article starts off describing the beginning of the dance in detail. But I didn't realize how quick Elijah's moves were. I am glad I got to see the dance myself, or I would have assumed the beginning was slower.

Skill: Informational Text Elements

This detail shows how Elijah got his unique style of dancing. The article talks about how Elijah's dancing is unusual, and this helps explain that he developed his style not from imitating other dancers but from imitating cartoons.

NOTES

NOTES

fast-forward and watch it fast and slow and try and imitate it. That's how I got started by watching their movements and seeing if I could do it," he says. "I didn't even start out dancing. I took what I learned from those cartoons and started doing magic tricks. I made those moves part of my magic act to make people laugh."

Planning for the Future

7 Although he's having fun, dancing is no laughing matter for Elijah, now that he has graduated from high school and is considering how he can **incorporate** dance into his life professionally. He hopes to attend Miami Dade College, and his dream job is in advertising, which would allow him to make commercials for a living.

8 "Everything happens for a reason and everything is connected," Elijah says. "I have a background in technology that I can use to my advantage. I can also pursue advertising. I don't see why my dancing has to stop. I can use my knowledge to teach dance classes online where I advertise and market the classes to students all over the world. There's a bridge that connects everything and I've found that bridge."

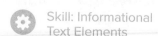

Skill: Informational
Text Elements

This is a pertinent detail about how Elijah is pursuing more practical things. Another central idea of the article is that Elijah is doing practical things in addition to dancing, and this shows me why he is doing that.

9 There's also his father, who is proud of his Elijah's dancing, but wants him to proceed with caution: "My dad wants me to have a back-up plan," Elijah says. "He says I need to have a degree and to do something I can fall back on if dance doesn't work out. He doesn't want me to give up on my dream, but he wants me to stay grounded."

A Well-rounded Education

10 YoungArts also helps Elijah pursue his dreams, which has been its goal since the National YoungArts Foundation opened its doors in 1981. Ted Arison, the businessman who created Carnival Cruise Lines, founded the nonprofit with his wife, Lin, the two of them believing that the best way to invest in the arts was to identify and nurture young artists such as Elijah.

11 One of the celebrated components of YoungArts is its strong community of 20,000-plus alumni, who encourage a lifetime of opportunity and support. Notable alumni include Kerry Washington, Anna Gunn, and Timothee Chalamet.

12 Although there is a heavy push for S.T.E.M. (science, technology, engineering and math) in schools, including the arts creates a well-rounded education, argues Arne Duncan, the former U.S. Secretary of Education. "As core

academic subjects, the arts and **humanities** equip young persons with the capacities to learn from the past, question the present, and envision new possibilities for the future," he says. "A well-rounded curriculum that embraces the arts and humanities is not a luxury but a necessity in the information age."

13   Aisha Brooks was Elijah's theater teacher at Miami Northwestern Senior High School, and although she has taught for 16 years, she says she will never forget Elijah and how well-rounded, enthusiastic, and confident he is.

14   "Elijah is very committed and creative," Brooks says. "He can do it all. He would choreograph dances and work with the students to create routines for our shows. And because he has a technical mind, he'd mix music for me and the chorus teacher, too. Elijah's not afraid to speak for himself. He was the one who was confident enough to speak up and tell me what he could do. But he also wasn't afraid to ask for help," Brooks adds. "If he could not do a move, he'd ask the dance teacher for help. He's going to go far in life."

15   As for the future, Elijah took classes at a few Miami dance studios, but yearned for more challenging routines—so he started his own dance team. Now he's learning new styles and touring and performing across the country, while also working with AmeriCorps to support himself and save money for college.

16   "Success does not come easily," Elijah says. "You have to work hard. You'll know you're doing what you're destined to do if things don't come easily. If there are constant roadblocks and problems, then you're on the right track."

First Read

Read "Miami Dancer Follows Dreams While Planning for the Future." After you read, complete the Think Questions below.

 THINK QUESTIONS

1. Describe Elijah's process for learning dance moves. Explain, using evidence from the text to support your answer.

2. What is Elijah's "bridge"—and what does it connect? Cite evidence from the text to support your answer.

3. Explain Elijah's father's attitude on his son's passion for dance. How do the visions of father and son overlap and diverge? Cite evidence from the text to support your response.

4. What is the meaning of the word **panache** as it is used in the text? Write your best definition here, along with a brief explanation of the context clues that helped you determine its meaning.

5. Use context clues to determine the meaning of the word **melancholy** as it is used in the text. Write your definition of *melancholy* here, and explain how you figured it out.

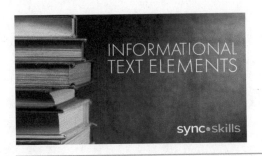

Skill:
Informational Text Elements

Use the Checklist to analyze Informational Text Elements in "Miami Dancer Follows Dreams While Planning for the Future." Refer to the sample student annotations about Informational Text Elements in the text.

••• CHECKLIST FOR INFORMATIONAL TEXT ELEMENTS

In order to identify the interactions between individuals, events, and ideas in a text, note the following:

- ✓ details in the text that describe or explain important ideas, events, or individuals

- ✓ transition words and phrases that signal interactions between individuals, ideas, or events, such as *because, as a consequence,* or *as a result*

- ✓ an event or sequence of events that influences an individual, a subsequent event, or an idea

- ✓ interactions between ideas and events that play a part in shaping people's thoughts and actions

To analyze the interactions between individuals, events, and ideas in a text, consider the following questions:

- ✓ How are the individuals, ideas, and events in the text related?

- ✓ How do the ideas the author presents affect the individuals in the text?

- ✓ What other features, if any, help readers to analyze the events, ideas, or individuals in the text?

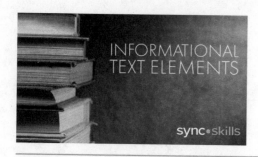

Skill:
Informational Text Elements

Reread paragraphs 13–15 of "Miami Dancer Follows Dreams While Planning for the Future." Then, using the Checklist on the previous page, answer the multiple-choice questions below.

⟳ YOUR TURN

1. This question has two parts. First, answer Part A. Then, answer Part B.

   Part A: What type of informational text element is in paragraph 14?

   ○ A. The list of the different things Elijah does for the school is supporting evidence for the claim in the previous paragraph.

   ○ B. The fact that Elijah is creative is a pertinent detail about the main idea of the whole article.

   ○ C. The detail that Elijah is not afraid to speak for himself supports the central idea in the following paragraph.

   ○ D. The evidence that Elijah is taking dance classes supports the idea in paragraph 13.

   Part B: Which of the following details BEST supports your response to Part A?

   ○ A. "but yearned for more challenging routines—so he started his own dance team."

   ○ B. "'Elijah is very committed and creative,' Brooks says."

   ○ C. "she says she will never forget Elijah and how well-rounded, enthusiastic, and confident he is"

   ○ D. "If he could not do a move, he'd ask the dance teacher for help. He's going to go far in life."

Skill:
Media

Use the Checklist to analyze Media in "Miami Dancer Follows Dreams While Planning for the Future." Refer to the sample student annotations about Media in the text.

••• CHECKLIST FOR MEDIA

In order to determine how to identify ideas presented in diverse media and formats, note the following:

✓ how the same topic can be treated, or presented, in more than one formats

- • visually
- • quantitatively
- • orally

✓ how treatments of a topic through different kinds of sources can reveal more information about the topic

✓ which details are emphasized or absent in each medium, and the reasons behind these choices

✓ what the details in each medium have in common, or the main idea in each medium

✓ how the main idea and supporting details help to clarify, or explain, a topic, text, or issue

In order to determine how to compare and contrast, analyze, or explain ideas presented in diverse media and formats, consider the following:

✓ How are the treatments of the source text similar? How are they different?

✓ How do ideas presented in diverse media and formats clarify, or explain, a topic, text, or issue?

✓ How does each medium's portrayal affect the presentation of the subject?

✓ Why are some media able to emphasize or highlight certain kinds of information better than others?

Please note that excerpts and passages in the StudySync® library and this workbook are intended as touchstones to generate interest in an author's work. The excerpts and passages do not substitute for the reading of entire texts, and StudySync® strongly recommends that students seek out and purchase the whole literary or informational work in order to experience it as the author intended. Links to online resellers are available in our digital library. In addition, complete works may be ordered through an authorized reseller by filling out and returning to StudySync® the order form enclosed in this workbook.

Reading & Writing Companion

63

Skill:
Media

Reread paragraphs 5–6 of "Miami Dancer Follows Dreams While Planning for the Future" and watch the video clip. Then, using the Checklist on the previous page, answer the multiple-choice questions below.

⟳ YOUR TURN

1. This question has two parts. First, answer Part A. Then, answer Part B.

   Part A: What can you see about Elijah's dancing in the video that reflects and clarifies what the writer says in the passage?

   ○ A. I can see that Elijah's dancing is classic and graceful.
   ○ B. I can tell from the video that Elijah was inspired by music videos.
   ○ C. The video shows me that Elijah didn't need to practice as much as the other dancers.
   ○ D. I can see how Elijah drew inspiration from things like cartoons.

   Part B: Which of the following details from the video BEST supports your response to Part A?

   ○ A. When Elijah falls down and moves his whole body to the heartbeat noise
   ○ B. The music Elijah chose for his performance
   ○ C. When Elijah spins on his knees
   ○ D. When Elijah moves and dances to the beat of the music

Close Read

Reread "Miami Dancer Follows Dreams While Planning for the Future." As you reread, complete the Skills Focus questions below. Then use your answers and annotations from the questions to help you complete the Write activity.

◎ SKILLS FOCUS

1. The title of this article implies that one of the main ideas is Elijah is a well-rounded student. Identify evidence that supports the idea that Elijah is a well-rounded student. Explain how that evidence relates to the main idea.

2. Elijah works hard to stand out. Identify pertinent examples that show how Elijah excelled through hard work. Explain how the evidence relates to Elijah's hard work.

3. The video that accompanies this article shows the dance that the article talks about. Identify elements from the medium that deepen your understanding of Elijah's dancing. Explain how the video adds to your understanding.

4. The author uses specific vocabulary to let the readers know what kind of person Elijah is. Identify words with emotional or positive connotations that help you understand Elijah. Explain how the connotation affects your understanding of Elijah.

5. Elijah is an outstanding young man in a lot of different ways. Identify evidence about how Elijah stands out from the crowd. Write a note about how the evidence shows Elijah standing out.

✏ WRITE

DEBATE: The article talks about how Elijah likes both STEM topics and the arts. Which do you think is more important? Is it more important to focus on science and technology or the arts and humanities? Prepare points and comments for a debate with your classmates. Use evidence from the text to support your point.

Please note that excerpts and passages in the StudySync® library and this workbook are intended as touchstones to generate interest in an author's work. The excerpts and passages do not substitute for the reading of entire texts, and StudySync® strongly recommends that students seek out and purchase the whole literary or informational work in order to experience it as the author intended. Links to online resellers are available in our digital library. In addition, complete works may be ordered through an authorized reseller by filling out and returning to StudySync® the order form enclosed in this workbook.

Reading & Writing Companion   65

Reality TV and Society

ARGUMENTATIVE TEXT
2014

Introduction

In these two articles, the writers make arguments for and against reality TV shows. One writer discusses the negative impacts of shows like *Jersey Shore* and *Here Comes Honey Boo Boo*, while the other focuses on the positive influence of shows like *American Idol* and *Supernanny*. Both writers present strong arguments and support their claims with evidence. Which of the arguments do

"Viewers see that people without talent or hard work can become rich and famous."

Reality TV Shows: Harmless entertainment or bad influence?

Point: Stop Rewarding Bad Behavior

1   Television has been an important part of American life for nearly seven decades. But instead of improving with age, programming has degenerated into mindless reality TV. Even though these programs claim to picture real people in real situations, there is actually very little *real* in reality TV. There is, however, a real **influence** on TV viewers, and this influence is often negative, especially on young people. Many people claim that reality TV portrays an accurate and vivid picture of our society. But if what Americans see on reality TV is truly who we are, then we are in big trouble.

2   According to Nielsen, a television ratings company, in 2014 nearly 300 million Americans ages two and up live in homes with televisions. That figure represents more than 90 percent of the population who have access to hundreds of channels and the programs they show. Unfortunately, ratings show that many television viewers are choosing *Here Comes Honey Boo Boo* over political talk shows, broadcasts of national political conventions, or other programming reflecting issues that affect us all.

3   Of course, reality TV has turned many people into instant celebrities. Viewers see that people without talent or hard work can become rich and famous. All they have to do is behave badly in front of the camera. But what message does this send to young people? According to Russ Rankin, who often writes for the arts, young people are not viewing reality TV as mindless entertainment. They look up to the programs' stars and imitate them. They are easily influenced by what they see, and they see that bad behavior is rewarded. Young viewers learn that those who treat others with pettiness and contempt become rich and famous. In fact, in 2011, one of the stars of *Jersey Shore* was paid more to address Rutgers University students than was Toni Morrison, a Nobel prize-winning author.

4   Tom Green is a comedian and actor who benefited from reality TV. Yet he is one of the most vocal voices against the genre. The difference for him, he

Skill: Arguments and Claims

This paragraph is about the people on reality TV. The Point author claims that reality TV stars convince people that bad behavior will make them famous. He supports this claim with the fact that reality stars get paid a lot. The author reasons that viewers learn that pettiness is rewarded.

Skill: Arguments
and Claims

This part also supports
the argument that
reality TV is harmful.
Here, the Point author
claims that the
networks need to take
responsibility for the
effects of reality TV.
The author then uses a
quote from Tom Green
and reasons that
networks should do
more to counteract the
harm caused by reality
TV. They've done similar
work to influence people
before.

says, is that he was not **exploited** and was in charge of his program. As the demand increased for more outrageous and negative programs, Green saw that "the audience became addicted to the cheap thrills." The quality of TV degenerated. He says, "The days of looking up to inventors, artists, and genuinely successful people are gone. Most people assume the behavior they see on TV is acceptable simply because it is on TV in the first place. Our media is shaping culture and training the audience to no longer demand quality programming. I had always presumed that the major corporations that ruled our media were far more responsible than I. Apparently, I was wrong."

5   Television producer Michael Slezak, senior editor of TVLine.com, says that he thinks reality TV shows are so prevalent because "networks love a good reality show since they're less expensive to produce. They don't require drawing in big stars."

6   It seems that no matter how often people are told that what they are watching is far from reality, they still watch. They continue to nurture false expectations that they too could become rich and famous if only they could be selected to participate in reality TV. In a recent survey, 10 percent of British teenagers were motivated by the dream of money and success. They said they would give up a good education to become a reality TV star.

7   It's not really the job of television networks to police the influences of television on culture and society. Yet networks do need to take some responsibility for what they have created with reality TV. As Tom Green says, "The networks should self-regulate by putting power back into the hands of artists and comedians." The media has done a massively good job of influencing society against smoking. They are now working on educating the public about obesity and healthy eating habits. They should be just as concerned about influencing the public about intelligent viewing and showing the best of how people should treat one another.

"These shows inspire young viewers. They see people like them succeeding."

Counterpoint: Reality TV Can Educate and Inspire

8   Which came first: the chicken or the egg? This age-old question can easily be applied to the **controversy** surrounding reality television. Have these shows **corrupted** our society? Or do they reflect the natural changes that have occurred in the way we see our world?

9   Most people who claim that reality TV has had a negative effect on society are mainly referring to shows that focus on celebrities such as *Keeping up with the Kardashians* or on contrived competitions such as *Survivor*. *Survivor* can be said to build teamwork, but the challenges the contestants face are admittedly not real. And even though the participants are not in any real danger, they are encouraged to create drama to thrill viewers.

10   Other competitive reality TV shows truly showcase talent. Programs such as *Project Runway, American Idol, America's Got Talent,* and *So You Think You Can Dance* give artists and performers the chance to appear before millions of TV viewers. As a result, the careers of many participants have been launched by way of these programs, even though these contestants did not win the competition. One dancer from Texas, for example, has danced professionally in music videos and on TV shows such as *Glee* since appearing on *So You Think You Can Dance*. These shows inspire young viewers. They see people like them succeeding. So they may think, "I can do that." In this way, reality shows encourage young people to reach for the stars.

NOTES

American Idol judges Lionel Richie, Katy Perry, and Luke Bryan, along with host Ryan Seacrest, search for America's next music sensation.

11   Reality shows that focus on the lives of everyday people may also give people comfort. As the Greek philosopher Aristotle once said of those who attended theater performances, they did so "to be cured, relieved, restored to psychic health." Viewers can identify with people who seem just like them. They see people with problems similar to (or worse than) their own. As a result, they may realize that their own struggles are not as bad as they thought.

12   Reality TV also introduces viewers to lifestyles, cultures, and people different from themselves. The NAACP reported in 2008 that reality programs are the only segment of television that fairly represents nonwhite groups. At least the people viewers see reflect the wide **diversity** of people in our nation.

13   Some reality TV shows actually improve society. For example, shows such as *Hoarders* increase public awareness of a serious mental health problem. Other shows, such as *Supernanny,* give parents and caregivers tips on how to handle children.

14   Blaming reality TV for society's challenges is a convenient way to avoid taking a hard look at ourselves and finding solutions to our problems. Life is messy, and reality TV honestly reveals that truth. Once we realize that we are far from perfect, we can learn to accept others for who they are. Certainly, acceptance of others, with all their faults, is a big step toward creating a better society for everyone.

First Read

Read "Reality TV and Society." After you read, complete the Think Questions below.

☁ THINK QUESTIONS

1. What position does the Point author take in the debate over reality TV? Cite two pieces of evidence from the Point essay to support your answer.

2. The Point author uses the opinion of comedian Tom Green to support the argument. How does Green's opinion help the author explain what has caused the quality of TV to decline? Cite specific evidence from paragraph 4 of the Point essay to support your answer.

3. What position does the Counterpoint author take in the debate over reality TV? Cite two pieces of evidence from paragraphs 12 and 13 to support your response.

4. Read the following dictionary entry:

cor·rupt /kə'rəpt/

verb

1. to cause to be dishonest or immoral in manners or actions
2. to cause errors or unintentional alterations to occur

adjective

1. dishonest for personal gain
2. evil or immoral
3. rotten or decaying

Which definition most closely matches the meaning of **corrupted** in paragraph 8? Write the correct definition of *corrupted* here and explain how you figured it out.

5. Use context clues to determine the meaning of the word **controversy** as it is used in the text. Write your definition of *controversy* here. Then look up the definition in an online or print dictionary to confirm or revise your meaning.

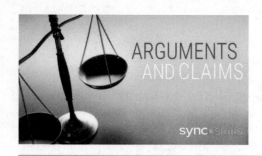

Skill:
Arguments and Claims

Use the Checklist to analyze Arguments and Claims in "Reality TV and Society." Refer to the sample student annotations about Arguments and Claims in the text.

••• CHECKLIST FOR ARGUMENTS AND CLAIMS

In order to trace the argument and specific claims, do the following:

- ✓ identify clues that reveal the author's opinion in the title, introduction, or conclusion

- ✓ note the first and last sentence of each body paragraph for specific claims that help to build the author's argument

- ✓ list the information the author introduces in sequential order

- ✓ use different colors to highlight and distinguish among an author's argument, claims, evidence, or reasons

- ✓ describe the author's argument in your own words

To evaluate the argument and specific claims, consider the following questions:

- ✓ Does the author support each claim with reasoning and evidence?

- ✓ Do the author's claims work together to support his or her overall argument?

- ✓ Which claims are not supported, if any?

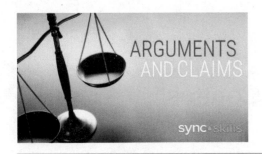

Skill:
Arguments and Claims

Reread paragraph 11 of the Counterpoint section and analyze the structure of the passage. Then, complete the chart below by identifying the claim in the passage as well as the reasoning behind the claim and the evidence that supports it.

⟳ YOUR TURN

Answer Bank	
A	Viewers who see people like themselves struggling may realize their problems are not so bad.
B	In Ancient Greece, watching people struggle helped people feel better and be "cured" or "restored."
C	Reality TV provides viewers with a sense of comfort and well-being.

Claim	Reason	Evidence

Skill:
Compare and Contrast

Use the Checklist to analyze Compare and Contrast in "Reality TV and Society."

In order to determine how two or more authors writing about the same topic shape their presentations of key information, use the following steps:

✓ first, choose two texts with similar subjects or topics by different authors

✓ next, identify each author's approach to the subject

✓ after, identify the key information and evidence each author includes

✓ then, explain the ways each author shapes the presentation of the information in the text

✓ finally, analyze the similarities and differences in how the authors present:

- key information
- evidence
- their interpretation of facts

To analyze how two or more authors writing about the same topic shape their presentations of key information, consider the following questions:

✓ In what ways do the texts I have chosen have similar subjects or topics?

✓ How does each author approach the topic or subject?

✓ How does each author's presentation of key information differ? How are they the same? How do these similarities and differences change the presentation and interpretation of the facts?

Skill:
Compare and Contrast

Reread paragraph 6 of the Point essay and paragraph 10 of the Counterpoint essay from "Reality TV and Society." Then, using the Checklist on the previous page, complete the chart below by sorting the observations to compare and contrast the passages.

↻ YOUR TURN

	Observations
A	Reality TV gives young people false expectations.
B	Reality TV makes people hope for fame and fortune.
C	Reality TV encourages young people to follow their dreams.
D	Reality TV inspires young people.
E	Reality TV influences young people.
F	Reality TV harms young people.

Point	Both	Counterpoint

Please note that excerpts and passages in the StudySync® library and this workbook are intended as touchstones to generate interest in an author's work. The excerpts and passages do not substitute for the reading of entire texts, and StudySync® strongly recommends that students seek out and purchase the whole literary or informational work in order to experience it as the author intended. Links to online resellers are available in our digital library. In addition, complete works may be ordered through an authorized reseller by filling out and returning to StudySync® the order form enclosed in this workbook.

Reading & Writing Companion

75

Close Read

Reread "Reality TV and Society." As you reread, complete the Skills Focus questions below. Then use your answers and annotations from the questions to help you complete the Write activity.

◎ SKILLS FOCUS

1. Identify details in the conclusion of each section of the article that connect to the section's claim. Explain how the conclusion of each section relates to the claim.

2. Identify reasons and evidence the writer uses to support a claim in the Point section. Explain how the reasons and evidence sufficiently support the claim.

3. Identify reasons and evidence the writer uses to support a claim in the Counterpoint section. Explain how the reasons and evidence sufficiently support the claim.

4. Compare and contrast the different authors' arguments. Identify pertinent examples and supporting evidence the authors use. Write a note explaining how the authors emphasize and explain the examples and evidence that support their arguments or claims.

5. Identify an example of how viewers, contestants, and participants interact with reality TV. Explain how reality TV reflects the human desire to stand out from the crowd.

✏ WRITE

DEBATE: With your classmates, debate whether reality TV is good or bad for society. To prepare for the debate, write your claim and provide three reasons with evidence to support your claim. Use examples from the text as well as from your own experience and research.

The Matsuyama Mirror

DRAMA
Velina Hasu Houston
1994

Introduction

Velina Hasu Houston (b. 1957) was born to an American father and Japanese mother—in an American household modeled after Japanese traditions. Today, she is a playwright, poet, essayist, and professor. In this excerpt from *The Matsuyama Mirror*, a Japanese man named Otoosan returns to his village of Matsuyama after a journey, bearing gifts for his family. But he also bears the news that his wife has died in a riding accident—news his daughters do not yet know. When he must give them the news about their mother, he tries to comfort their grief with reassurances and gifts. Aiko's gift, in particular, proves to be very

"Are you not curious about your present, Aiko?"

CAST OF CHARACTERS

AIKO
TOORIKO
OKAASAN (also GRAND MISTRESS OF MATSUYAMA)
OTOOSAN
YUKIKO OBASAN
Aiko's Chorus of Dolls: FIRST KOKESHI
                       SECOND KOKESHI
                       THIRD KOKESHI

NOTE

One Kuro-ko (stage assistant in Japanese tradition) is needed. This responsibility can be carried out by any actor in the company.

SETTING

1600s. Matsuyama, Japan; and a magical world.

. . .

1   *(Sounds of horses are heard from off stage. Aiko tries to run out, but is stopped by OTOOSAN who enters covered with snow. He conceals **grimness** with a smile for his children. He carries a satchel[1] filled to **capacity**.)*

2   OTOOSAN: Good daughters. Hello.

3   TOORIKO: *(Bowing low)* Welcome home, Otoosan.

4   AIKO: Welcome, Father.

5   OTOOSAN: Where are you going in such a hurry, Aiko?

6   TOORIKO: Out into the snow to find you!

---

1. **satchel** a bag, typically carried over the shoulder

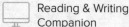

NOTES

7 AIKO: Where is Mother?

8 OTOOSAN: It is so cold. Let me sit for a—

9 AIKO: Is she with the horses?

10 TOORIKO: Quiet, Aiko!

11 *(Tooriko helps him off with his coat. He and Tooriko sit around the candle. Incredulous, Aiko puts on her father's coat and prepares to leave.)*

12 OTOOSAN: Take off my coat and sit, Aiko.

13 AIKO: Tell me where she is.

14 OTOOSAN: Sit.

15 *(Otoosan takes the coat off of her and forces her to sit.)*

16 Children, your mother has . . . left us.

17 AIKO: What? No. No.

18 OTOOSAN: . . . there has been . . . an accident.

19 *(The breath knocked out of her, Aiko sits motionlessly. Tooriko is quiet with shock for a moment and then weeps uncontrollably.)*

20 AIKO: **(Eerie** calmness) You must tell me what has happened to my mother.

21 OTOOSAN: The snow. An accident with the horses. Her head struck a rock. When they found her, she was already . . .

22 AIKO: How can you sit there like a piece of stone?

23 TOORIKO: Aiko!

24 AIKO: How can you? What are you?

25 OTOOSAN: The bearer of our pain so that you can go on.

26 TOORIKO: Oh, this family. Pull yourself together, Father.

27 OTOOSAN: Your mother drifts in the winds tonight, seeking her next existence. We must keep the sky clear; we must not weep.

Skill:
Word Meaning

I am not sure what the word drifts means, but I can tell it's a verb. Drifts is what the mother or her spirit is doing tonight. There are more verbs that show the family's reaction to the mother's death and her spirit drifting. Otoosan says they must keep the sky clear, and Aiko asks for her mother to come back. I wonder if these will help me understand the meaning of drifts in this line?

NOTES

28 AIKO: Bring her back. *(To the ether)* Come back, Okaasan. Come back! Please, please, come back.

29 OTOOSAN: Enough, gentle Aiko-chan . . . we must go on as usual . . .

30 AIKO: What? How?

31 TOORIKO: Shall we sit around like fools and weep?

32 AIKO: You never loved her like I did.

33 TOORIKO: I am older and I have loved her longer.

34 AIKO: And I love her best.

35 *(Otoosan reaches for the satchel and removes two packages.)*

36 OTOOSAN: Here. Your gifts. Come. Let us be as curious and happy as we always are when I return from my journeys.

37 AIKO: I only want the return of my mother.

38 OTOOSAN: What do you think I brought you, Aiko-chan?

39 AIKO: Who will I ask for help when I am learning new embroidery[2]?

40 TOORIKO: I will help you.

41 AIKO: You do not help. You order.

42 OTOOSAN: We will all help each other.

43 AIKO: Tooriko-san will only help herself and her husband.

44 TOORIKO: What is wrong with that? If you ever grow up, you will bring a husband to live here with you and Otoosan. You will know secrets that will make you selfish sometimes, too.

45 OTOOSAN: Yes, Aiko, I will find you a strong, patient man.

46 TOORIKO: In this case, perhaps a saint is required.

47 OTOOSAN: And Tooriko will always be near. Her husband plans to build their new house just on the other side of the village.

Skill:
Media

When I was reading it, I thought that this scene was just two sisters bickering. When I listened to the audio version, though, I thought the scene was funny. Tooriko's line could have just been mean, but the actor makes it comedic with her performance.

---

2. **embroidery** decorative cloth with designs sewn into it with thread

NOTES

48   AIKO: It might as well be on the other side of the universe.

49   OTOOSAN: When I am gone, you two sisters will be all that is left of our family. Can you not be **civil** to one another? Come, Aiko-chan. Come sit by me.

50   AIKO: Who will cook tonight, Otoosan?

51   TOORIKO: I will cook.

52   AIKO: You? The taste will kill— Sorry. But you don't know how to cook. You don't.

53   OTOOSAN: Your aunt will come tomorrow to help.

54   AIKO: Aunt Yukiko!

55   OTOOSAN: This is a time to find strength in family. Yukiko Obasan is good and kind.

56   AIKO: And rough as a tree trunk.

57   TOORIKO: But sturdy and lasting.

58   OTOOSAN: Are you not curious about your present, Aiko? Perhaps it will give you a little light in this darkness?

59   AIKO: *(Facetiously)* Oh I am certain.

60   OTOOSAN: Then if I have brought a new doll, must I find another little girl to give it to?

61   AIKO: Otoosan? Could the gods have made a mistake? Can they be persuaded to give back my mother?

62   OTOOSAN: Open your present, dear child.

63   AIKO: How can I behold these gifts at such a time?

64   TOORIKO: Because we need to. If I stare at the tatami[3] all night and cry, then I will not make it to morning.

65   OTOOSAN: Here, Tooriko-san.

66   *(She opens her gift. It is a scarf.)*

---

3. **tatami** a straw mat forming a traditional Japanese floor covering

67 TOORIKO: Thank you, Otoosan. I shall save it.

68 OTOOSAN: Do not save it. Wear it. Make yourself look beautiful. Today. Now. And for you, Aiko-chan.

69 *(He takes out a silver, sparkling box. Immediately, the Kuro-ko tinkles wind chimes and Aiko looks around, startled as if she hears something. Aiko holds the box and slowly opens it, scattering sparkling dust. She takes out a large silver and gold lacquered mirror with angel hair hanging in shreds from it. It leaves her in a state of awe. Tooriko is afraid of it.)*

70 AIKO: What is it, Father?

71 OTOOSAN: It is called a "mirror."

72 AIKO: ". . . mirror . . ."

73 TOORIKO: Does it belong in the house?

74 OTOOSAN: It is magic. Look in the glass.

75 AIKO: *(Startled)* There is a girl in the glass!

76 OTOOSAN: *(Laughs)* And who does she look like?

77 *(Aiko dares look again and gasps. Tooriko's curiosity is quelled by fear.)*

78 AIKO: It is Mother, when she was a young girl!

79 *(Tooriko screams in fright and Otoosan silences her with a gentle look.)*

80 OTOOSAN: It seems so, does it not?

81 AIKO: Mother has become a child in this mirror. How can that be so? What have you done? Have you put her in the mirror? Can I get her out?

82 TOORIKO: No! No! We will all be cursed.

83 OTOOSAN: Whenever you miss your mother, look in this mirror and you will find her looking back at you.

84 *(Warm, loving woman's laughter is heard only by Aiko who jumps in surprise and fear.)*

85 TOORIKO: *(Staring at her)* You are possessed.

86 AIKO: There is a spirit in the mirror! I can hear her; can you hear—

87 OTOOSAN: No one else in Matsuyama has such a mirror. You will be the talk of the town.

88 TOORIKO: And not just because of this mirror.

89 *(Aiko brandishes the mirror toward her sister who jumps in fright.)*

90 Keep that thing away from me! It is black magic.

91 OTOOSAN: It is healing magic.

92 *(Removes a porcelain doll from his satchel.)*

93 I brought this porcelain doll for your mother.

94 *(He offers it to Tooriko, but she motions for him to offer it to Aiko. He hands it to Aiko. Her **pleasure** gives Tooriko pleasure.)*

95 For you, Aiko-chan.

96 AIKO: Thank you, Otoosan.

97 *(He picks up his things and leaves. Tooriko tries to blow out the candle and Aiko stops her.)*

98 Leave it be.

99 TOORIKO: But it is almost burned away. There is no use for it.

100 AIKO: Let it burn and, when it is gone, I want its scent to linger in my hair and kimono.

101 TOORIKO: Little sister, learn to be practical. As you can see, our parents are not immortal.

102 AIKO: But they are. Mother lives. I saw her in this mirror.

103 TOORIKO: Put that thing away!

104 AIKO: But I really saw her. I did!

105 TOORIKO: Aiko-chan, childhood is a butterfly feeding on the dew of youth. And the dew disappears quickly. You must grow up.

106   AIKO: No. Never-never-no.

107   TOORIKO: Oh, how can you behave so when she has died this night? Do you not see that the gods have punished her for riding out into the snow like a soldier?

108   AIKO: She is a soldier, a soldier of the soul, like me! I shall ride, too, and I will return in one piece with Mother at my side.

109   TOORIKO: Dear Aiko . . . Good night.

110   AIKO: The night shall never be good again.

111   *(Tooriko leaves. Aiko stares into the mirror as the Kuro-ko tinkles the wind chimes. Lights crossfade . . .)*

By Velina Hasu Houston, 2015. Published by and performances licensed through YouthPLAYS (https://www.youthplays.com). Reproduced by permission of YouthPLAYS.

First Read

Read *The Matsuyama Mirror*. After you read, complete the Think Questions below.

☁ THINK QUESTIONS

1. This play takes place in a setting in which nobody has ever seen a mirror before. When Tooriko exclaims that the mirror is "black magic," Otoosan corrects her by saying that it is "healing magic." What does he mean by this? Why would he decide that Aiko needed this magic more than her sister or himself? Cite the text to support your answer.

2. At the end of this scene, Tooriko tries to blow out the candle lighting their home, but Aiko stops her, even though she has no practical need for the candle. What might be the reason for this? Use what you know about Aiko's character to speculate a couple of possibilities.

3. Although the two sisters seem to have a difficult relationship, there are moments in the dialogue and stage directions that hint that each feels a sisterly love for the other. Find them and list them here.

4. Use context clues to determine the meaning of the word **civil** as it is used in the play. Write your definition of *civil* here, along with the parts of the text that helped you arrive at that definition. Then check a dictionary to confirm your understanding.

5. The roots of the noun **capacity** are the Latin word *capiō,* which means "to hold/contain," and the Latin suffix *-itās,* which is used to create the noun form of other words that are adjectives or verbs. Keeping these roots in mind, write a definition of *capacity* as it appears in the text, and explain how your knowledge of its root words helped you arrive at that meaning.

Please note that excerpts and passages in the StudySync® library and this workbook are intended as touchstones to generate interest in an author's work. The excerpts and passages do not substitute for the reading of entire texts, and StudySync® strongly recommends that students seek out and purchase the whole literary or informational work in order to experience it as the author intended. Links to online resellers are available in our digital library. In addition, complete works may be ordered through an authorized reseller by filling out and returning to StudySync® the order form enclosed in this workbook.

Reading & Writing Companion 85

Skill:
Word Meaning

Use the Checklist to analyze Word Meaning in *The Matsuyama Mirror*. Refer to the sample student annotations about Word Meaning in the text.

••• CHECKLIST FOR WORD MEANING

In order to find the pronunciation of a word or determine or clarify its precise meaning or its part of speech, do the following:

- ✓ try to determine the word's part of speech from the context

- ✓ consult reference materials, both print and digital, to find the pronunciation of a word or determine or clarify its precise meaning or its part of speech

- ✓ consult general and specialized reference materials, both print and digital, to find the pronunciation of a word or determine or clarify its precise meaning or its part of speech

In order to verify the preliminary determination of the meaning of a word or phrase, do the following:

- ✓ use context clues to make an inference about the word's meaning

- ✓ consult a dictionary to verify your preliminary determination of the meaning

- ✓ be sure to read all of the definitions, and then decide which definition makes sense within the context of the text

To determine a word's precise meaning or part of speech, ask the following questions:

- ✓ What is the word describing?

- ✓ How is the word being used in the phrase or sentence?

- ✓ Have I consulted my reference materials?

Skill:
Word Meaning

Reread the stage directions and lines 97–101 from *The Matsuyama Mirror* and the dictionary entries below. Use the dictionary entry to determine the meaning, word origin, and part of speech. Then, using the Checklist from the previous page, answer the multiple-choice questions that follow.

♻ YOUR TURN

linger \ˈlin-gər\ *verb*

1: to be slow in parting or in quitting something
2: to remain alive although gradually dying
3: to remain existent although often waning in strength, importance, or influence
4: to be slow to act

Origin: from Middle English *lengeren* "to dwell"

1. Which definition best matches the word *linger* as used in line 100? Remember to pay attention to the word's part of speech as you make your decision.

   ○ A. Definition 2
   ○ B. Definition 4
   ○ C. Definition 1
   ○ D. Definition 3

Please note that excerpts and passages in the StudySync® library and this workbook are intended as touchstones to generate interest in an author's work. The excerpts and passages do not substitute for the reading of entire texts, and StudySync® strongly recommends that students seek out and purchase the whole literary or informational work in order to experience it as the author intended. Links to online resellers are available in our digital library. In addition, complete works may be ordered through an authorized reseller by filling out and returning to StudySync® the order form enclosed in this workbook.

Reading & Writing Companion   **87**

immortal \(,)i-mor-tel\

adjective

1: exempt from death
2: exempt from oblivion
3: connected with or relating to immortality

noun

4: one exempt from death
5: a person whose fame is lasting

Origin: from Middle English, from Latin *immortalis,* from *in-* + *mortalis*

2. Which definition best matches the way the word *immortal* is used in line 101? Remember to use the word's part of speech as you make your decision.

- ○ A. Definition 1
- ○ B. Definition 4
- ○ C. Definition 2
- ○ D. Definition 5

Skill:
Media

Use the Checklist to analyze Media in *The Matsuyama Mirror*. Refer to the sample student annotations about Media in the text.

••• CHECKLIST FOR MEDIA

In order to determine how to compare and contrast a written story, drama, or poem to its audio, filmed, staged, or multimedia version, do the following:

✓ choose a story that has been presented in multiple forms of media, such as a written story and a film adaptation

✓ note techniques that are unique to each medium—print, audio, and video:

- sound
- music
- tone and style
- word choice
- structure

✓ examine how these techniques may have an effect on the story and its ideas, as well as the reader's, listener's, or viewer's understanding of the work as a whole

✓ examine similarities and differences between the written story and its audio or video version

To compare and contrast a written story, drama, or poem to its audio, filmed, staged, or multimedia version, analyzing the effects of techniques unique to each medium, consider the following questions:

✓ How do different types of media treat story elements?

✓ What techniques are unique to each medium—print, audio, and video?

✓ How does the medium—for example, a film's use of music, sound, and camera angles—affect a person's understanding of the work as a whole?

Skill:
Media

Reread lines 50–57 of the play and listen to the audio clip. Use the Checklist on the previous page, to determine the answers to the multiple-choice questions

↻ YOUR TURN

1. This question has two parts. First, answer Part A. Then, answer Part B.

   Part A: How does the audio version help you understand the character of Aiko in this clip?

   ○ A. I can tell Aiko is stubborn.
   ○ B. I can tell that she loves her aunt.
   ○ C. I can tell that Aiko is funny.
   ○ D. I can tell that Aiko is sad.

   Part B: Which of the following performances from the audio clip BEST supports your response to Part A?

   ○ A. AIKO: Sorry. But you don't know how to cook. You don't.
   ○ B. AIKO: And rough as a tree trunk.
   ○ C. OTOOSAN: This is a time to find strength in family.
   ○ D. AIKO: Aunt Yukiko!

Close Read

Reread *The Matsuyama Mirror.* As you reread, complete the Skills Focus questions below. Then use your answers and annotations from the questions to help you complete the Write activity.

◎ SKILLS FOCUS

1. The characters in this story experience a great loss. How do the plot elements reveal aspects of the characters to the reader?

2. Dramatic elements help set the scene of a play and give the reader information about what they would see and hear at the show. How do the stage directions help you understand the tone of the play?

3. Think back to the audio recording of the play. How did the sound elements affect your understanding of the characters and tone of the play?

4. Aiko does not feel like she fits in with her family. What about Aiko makes her stand out? How does the play support the idea that Aiko is outstanding?

✏ WRITE

LITERARY ANALYSIS: Listening to a performance of a play is a different experience than reading the script. How do the sound elements affect your understanding of the characters? Use specific examples from the text and the audio to show how the audio contributes to your understanding of the characters.

Please note that excerpts and passages in the StudySync® library and this workbook are intended as touchstones to generate interest in an author's work. The excerpts and passages do not substitute for the reading of entire texts, and StudySync® strongly recommends that students seek out and purchase the whole literary or informational work in order to experience it as the author intended. Links to online resellers are available in our digital library. In addition, complete works may be ordered through an authorized reseller by filling out and returning to StudySync® the order form enclosed in this workbook.

Reading & Writing Companion   91

New Directions

INFORMATIONAL TEXT
Maya Angelou
1993

Introduction

Maya Angelou (1928–2014) was an American poet, essayist, and activist best known for her heralded autobiography, *I Know Why the Caged Bird Sings*. "New Directions" is another well-known nonfiction piece by Angelou. In this biographical essay, she recounts the life of her grandmother, Annie Johnson. When Annie's marriage ended in 1903, she realized that she must work in order to support her two small boys. As an African American woman, her choices were limited, yet Annie "cuts a new path" for herself through hard work and resourcefulness. In sharing her grandmother's story, Angelou teaches readers a

"She had indeed stepped from the road which seemed to have been chosen for her . . ."

1 In 1903 the late Mrs. Annie Johnson of Arkansas found herself with two toddling sons, very little money, a slight ability to read and add simple numbers. To this picture add a disastrous marriage and the **burdensome** fact that Mrs. Johnson was a Negro.

2 When she told her husband, Mr. William Johnson, of her dissatisfaction with their marriage, he **conceded** that he too found it to be less than he expected, and had been secretly hoping to leave and study religion. He added that he thought God was calling him not only to preach but to do so in Enid, Oklahoma. He did not tell her that he knew a minister in Enid with whom he could study and who had a friendly, unmarried daughter. They parted amicably, Annie keeping the one-room house and William taking most of the cash to carry himself to Oklahoma.

3 Annie, over six feet tall, big-boned, decided that she would not go to work as a **domestic** and leave her "precious babes" to anyone else's care. There was no possibility of being hired at the town's cotton gin[1] or lumber mill[2], but maybe there was a way to make the two factories work for her. In her words, "I looked up the road I was going and back the way I come, and since I wasn't satisfied, I decided to step off the road and cut me a new path." She told herself that she wasn't a fancy cook but that she could "mix groceries well enough to scare hungry away and from starving a man."

4 She made her plans **meticulously** and in secret. One early evening to see if she was ready, she placed stones in two five-gallon pails and carried them three miles to the cotton gin. She rested a little, and then, discarding some rocks, she walked in the darkness to the saw mill[3] five miles farther along the dirt road. On her way back to her little house and her babies, she dumped the remaining rocks along the path.

---

1. **cotton gin** a machine that separates cotton from seeds
2. **lumber mill** a factory where timber is cut into rough planks
3. **saw mill** a factory in which logs are sawed into lumber

Reading & Writing Companion

5   That same night she worked into the early hours boiling chicken and frying ham. She made dough and filled the rolled-out pastry with meat. At last she went to sleep.

6   The next morning she left her house carrying the meat pies, lard, an iron brazier, and coals for a fire. Just before lunch she appeared in an empty lot behind the cotton gin. As the dinner noon bell rang, she dropped the savors[4] into boiling fat and the aroma rose and floated over to the workers who spilled out of the gin, covered with white lint, looking like specters[5].

7   Most workers had brought their lunches of pinto beans and biscuits or crackers, onions and cans of sardines, but they were tempted by the hot meat pies which Annie ladled out of the fat. She wrapped them in newspapers, which soaked up the grease, and offered them for sale at a nickel each. Although business was slow, those first days Annie was determined. She balanced her appearances between the two hours of activity.

8   So, on Monday if she offered hot fresh pies at the cotton gin and sold the remaining cooled-down pies at the lumber mill for three cents, then on Tuesday she went first to the lumber mill presenting fresh, just-cooked pies as the lumbermen covered in sawdust emerged from the mill.

9   For the next few years, on balmy spring days, blistering summer noon, and cold, wet, and wintry middays, Annie never disappointed her customers, who could count on seeing the tall, brown-skin woman bent over her brazier, carefully turning the meat pies. When she felt certain that the workers had become dependent on her, she built a stall between the two hives of industry and let the men run to her for their lunchtime provisions.

10   She had indeed stepped from the road which seemed to have been chosen for her and cut herself a brand-new path. In years that stall became a store where customers could buy cheese, meal, syrup, cookies, candy, writing tablets, pickles, canned goods, fresh fruit, soft drinks, coal, oil, and leather soles for worn-out shoes.

11   Each of us has the right and the responsibility to **assess** the roads which lie ahead, and those over which we have traveled, and if the future road looms **ominous** or unpromising, and the roads back uninviting, then we need to gather our resolve and, carrying only the necessary baggage, step off that road into another direction. If the new choice is also unpalatable, without embarrassment, we must be ready to change that as well.

---

4. **savors** flavors or seasonings
5. **specters** ghosts or spirits

"New Directions" from WOULDN'T TAKE NOTHING FOR MY JOURNEY NOW by Maya Angelou, copyright ©1993 by Maya Angelou. Used by permission of Random House, an imprint and division of Random House LLC. All rights reserved.

NOTES

✏ WRITE

PERSONAL RESPONSE: What does author Maya Angelou think of her grandmother? Why do you think she tells her grandmother's story? Write a response to these questions. Remember to use evidence from the text to support your response.

Please note that excerpts and passages in the StudySync® library and this workbook are intended as touchstones to generate interest in an author's work. The excerpts and passages do not substitute for the reading of entire texts, and StudySync® strongly recommends that students seek out and purchase the whole literary or informational work in order to experience it as the author intended. Links to online resellers are available in our digital library. In addition, complete works may be ordered through an authorized reseller by filling out and returning to StudySync® the order form enclosed in this workbook.

Reading & Writing Companion   **95**

Choices

POETRY
Nikki Giovanni
1978

Introduction

Nikki Giovanni (b. 1943) calls herself a "Black American, a daughter, a mother, a professor of English." She is also the recipient of 25 honorary degrees, as well as an award-winning poet, writer, and activist who gives voice to issues of social justice and identity. Her poem "Choices" speaks to her inner struggle to make the best of any situation, especially when faced with limitations. Rather than quitting or dwelling on her limitations, she "chooses" to act, think, and move in some way—and, in doing so, chooses to pursue her own personal progress.

"it's not the same thing
but it's the best i can do"

1 if i can't do
2 what i want to do
3 then my job is to not
4 do what i don't want
5 to do

6 it's not the same thing
7 but it's the best i can
8 do

9 if i can't have
10 what i want . . . then
11 my job is to want
12 what i've got
13 and be **satisfied**
14 that at least there
15 is something more
16 to want

17 since i can't go
18 where i need
19 to go . . . then i must . . . go
20 where the signs point
21 though always understanding
22 **parallel** movement
23 isn't **lateral**

  Skill: Poetic Elements and Structure

The poem is written in open verse, without a fixed rhyme scheme or meter. However, the repetition of the word "do" creates a rhythm and emphasizes action. This contributes to the poem's meaning about making choices.

The repetition of "do" expresses the idea of active choice in the poem. Placing "not" at the end of a line emphasizes this word and expresses the idea of using free will and making choices despite limitations.

24   when i can't **express**
25   what i really feel
26   i practice feeling
27   what i can express
28   and none of it is **equal**
29   i know
30   but that's why mankind
31   alone among the mammals
32   learns to cry

CHOICES

First Read

Read "Choices." After you read, complete the Think Questions below.

☁ THINK QUESTIONS

1. According to the first stanza, what is the speaker's "job"?

2. What are the speaker's feelings about satisfaction and wanting? Cite evidence from the third stanza to support your answer.

3. Does the speaker feel free to fully express her feelings? Cite evidence from the final stanza in your response.

4. Read the following dictionary entry:

   parallel par•al•lel \'per ə, lel\
   noun

   1. something that is similar or comparable to something else

   verb

   1. to remain side by side with something in a line

   adjective

   1. side-by-side at a distance that is continuously the same

   Which definition most closely matches the meaning of **parallel** as it is used in line 22? Write the correct definition of *parallel* here and explain how you figured out the proper meaning.

5. Read the following dictionary entry:

   express ex•press \ik'spres\
   verb

   1. to represent using a number or formula
   2. to say or make known

   adjective

   1. happening quickly or at a high speed
   2. stated directly or explicitly

   Which definition most closely matches the meaning of **express** as it is used in line 24? Write the correct definition of *express* here and explain how you figured out the proper meaning.

Please note that excerpts and passages in the StudySync® library and this workbook are intended as touchstones to generate interest in an author's work. The excerpts and passages do not substitute for the reading of entire texts, and StudySync® strongly recommends that students seek out and purchase the whole literary or informational work in order to experience it as the author intended. Links to online resellers are available in our digital library. In addition, complete works may be ordered through an authorized reseller by filling out and returning to StudySync® the order form enclosed in this workbook.

Reading & Writing Companion

99

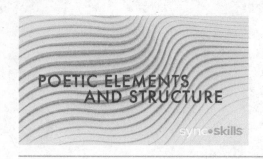

Skill: Poetic Elements and Structure

Use the Checklist to analyze Poetic Elements and Structure in "Choices." Refer to the sample student annotations about Poetic Elements and Structure in the text.

In order to identify poetic elements and structure, note the following:

- ✓ the form and overall structure of the poem

- ✓ the rhyme, rhythm and meter, if present

- ✓ other sound elements, such as:

  • alliteration: the repetition of initial consonant sounds, as with the *s* sound in "Cindy sweeps the sand"

- ✓ lines and stanzas in the poem that suggest its meaning

- ✓ ways that the poem's form or structure connects to the poem's meaning

To analyze how a drama's or poem's form or structure contributes to its meaning, consider the following questions:

- ✓ What poetic form does the poet use? What is the structure?

- ✓ How do the lines and stanzas and their length affect the meaning?

- ✓ How do the form and structure contribute to the poem's meaning?

To analyze the impact of rhymes and other repetitions of sounds on a specific verse or stanza of a poem, consider the following questions:

- ✓ What sound elements are present in specific stanzas of the poem?

- ✓ What is the effect of different sound elements on the stanza or verse?

POETIC ELEMENTS
AND STRUCTURE

sync•skills

Skill: Poetic
Elements and Structure

Reread lines 6–8 of "Choices." Then, using the Checklist on the previous page, answer the multiple-choice questions below.

↻ YOUR TURN

1. The third line contains only one word, "do." The reader can conclude that —

   ○ A. this is not an important line.

   ○ B. this word is being emphasized.

   ○ C. there was not enough room on the previous line.

   ○ D. the poet was not very careful when writing.

2. Lines 6–8 are important to the poem because they —

   ○ A. include a lowercase "i" to show that the speaker feels powerless and cannot make a choice.

   ○ B. express the theme that it is important to make choices even when there are limitations.

   ○ C. help to establish the regular rhyme scheme and meter of this poem.

   ○ D. convey the idea that one's best effort is not always good enough.

Please note that excerpts and passages in the StudySync® library and this workbook are intended as touchstones to generate interest in an author's work. The excerpts and passages do not substitute for the reading of entire texts, and StudySync® strongly recommends that students seek out and purchase the whole literary or informational work in order to experience it as the author intended. Links to online resellers are available in our digital library. In addition, complete works may be ordered through an authorized reseller by filling out and returning to StudySync® the order form enclosed in this workbook.

Reading & Writing
Companion

101

Close Read

Reread "Choices." As you reread, complete the Skills Focus questions below. Then use your answers and annotations from the questions to help you complete the Write activity.

◎ SKILLS FOCUS

1. Identify the use of repetition in the third stanza. Explain how these elements impact the meaning of the poem.

2. Identify the use of repetition and spacing in the fourth stanza. Explain how these elements and structures help you to understand what the poet is trying to say.

3. Identify a detail in the fifth stanza that develops the theme of the poem and explain how the detail supports the theme.

4. The speaker faces limitations but continues to value her individuality. How does the poem suggest that we stand out from the crowd?

✏ WRITE

COMPARE AND CONTRAST: In "New Directions," Maya Angelou tells the story of how her grandmother started a career for herself to support her family. It has an important message about overcoming obstacles and creating a new path for yourself. How does Nikki Giovanni use poetic elements and structure to express a similar message or theme? Use evidence from the text to support your answer.

Cuentos de Josefina
(Josephine's Tales)

DRAMA
Gregory Ramos
2016

Introduction

Cuentos de Josefina (Josephine's Tales) is a collection of interconnected plays by Gregory Ramos, narrated by young Josefina and her little brother, Ignacio. The two of them tell stories and folktales that weave together Mexican folklore with modern settings and situations, exploring what it means to leave one land in search of another, and the value in maintaining ties to one's past. The short play excerpted here, "The Tale of the Haunted Squash," is a story of greed and superstition. Read along as Josefina and Ignacio tell the tale of a young couple, Filiberto and Elvira, who disobey an agreement and reap the rewards—but only at a certain cost.

"Maybe I wasn't born under a lucky star after all."

NOTES

CHARACTERS:

JOSIE, female.
JOSEFINA, female.
YOUNG JOSEFINA, female. Age 15.
IGNACIO, male. Age 11.
FILIBERTO, male.
ELVIRA, female.
LA TÍA, female.
SEÑOR TRUJILLO, male.
EL ESQUELETO, any gender.
NEIGHBOR, any gender.
OLD MAN (RODOLFO), male.
GUESTS 1–4, any gender.
ACTORS 5–8, any gender.

TALE 2: THE TALE OF THE HAUNTED SQUASH

1   YOUNG JOSEFINA: Filiberto and his wife Elvira faced hard times.

2   (*FILIBERTO and ELVIRA enter with meager belongings.*)

3   IGNACIO: There was a drought. And they were forced to leave their *pueblito* (village).

4   YOUNG JOSEFINA: On the train, leaving the village, Filiberto played a high stakes card game.

5   (*Actors assemble for card game.*)

6   IGNACIO: Desperate to improve their situation, he bet the few pesos that he and Elvira had saved.

7   ELVIRA: Filiberto, no!!!

8   YOUNG JOSEFINA: But—he won! And lost! And won! And lost. And finally . . .

Copyright © BookheadEd Learning, LLC

9   FILIBERTO: I won the deed to land!

10   *(SEÑOR TRUJILLO and Filiberto sign deed. They shake hands.)*

11   *Gracias* (Thank you), Señor Trujillo.

12   *(Elvira inspects the deed as Señor Trujillo slinks away.)*

13   ELVIRA: *(Suddenly:) Mira!* (Look!) There's a **clause** here that says we're forbidden to plant in the west garden. Why?

14   FILIBERTO: Who cares? It's a house and ten acres and it's ours! *Híjole*[1]! My mother always said I was born under a lucky star.

15   YOUNG JOSEFINA: So, Filiberto and Elvira settled into their new house. Elvira made bread in the kitchen and peddled it on the streets, but there was a lot of competition. Filiberto planted tomatoes, carrots and lettuces only in the east garden. They grew, but they were puny and sickly and he tried to sell them.

16   *(Elvira and Filiberto count their earnings at the end of the day.)*

17   ELVIRA: Ten, eleven, twelve *centavos*[2]. That's all?

18   FILIBERTO: I tell you, no one wants my vegetables. They're puny and sickly.

19   ELVIRA: If we could only plant in the west garden. The soil there is so rich.

20   FILIBERTO: We can't.

21   ELVIRA: Why not?

22   FILIBERTO: We signed an agreement.

23   ELVIRA: Who's going to know?

24   FILIBERTO: Elvira!

25   YOUNG JOSEFINA: *(Narrating:)* That next day, Elvira did not make bread to peddle on the streets. Instead, while Filiberto was peddling his puny vegetables in the market, she went into town, bought a bag of *calabaza* (pumpkin) seeds and spent the entire day in the warm sun sowing the seeds in the west garden.

---

1. *Híjole!* an expression used to express surprise
2. **centavos** a monetary unit equal to one hundredth of the basic unit

Skill: Dramatic Elements and Structure

Elvira and Filiberto are talking to each other, but Josefina is talking to the audience. Josefina is telling the audience about the plot so we know what is happening. She lets us know that both characters are having problems. Maybe these problems will be related to the play's lesson?

NOTES

26 *(Elvira sows seeds. End of day, she's spent.)*

27 FILIBERTO: Elvira, I'm home.

28 *(Elvira cleans up quickly and runs into the house.)*

29 Here's the money from today's sales.

30 ELVIRA: (*Counting:*) Five, ten, fourteen, fifteen *centavos*. That's all?

31 FILIBERTO: How did the bread sales go today?

32 ELVIRA: How do you think? Lousy. If only we could . . .

33 FILIBERTO: No!

34 ELVIRA: But we're barely surviving!

35 FILIBERTO: Maybe I wasn't born under a lucky star after all.

36 *(He starts off, deflated.)*

37 ELVIRA: Filiberto . . .

38 *(Rooster [actor] crows.)*

39 YOUNG JOSEFINA: But . . . the next morning, Filiberto and Elvira discovered something in the west garden.

40 *(Filiberto stands in the west garden surrounded by* calabazas *[pumpkins].)*

41 FILIBERTO: Elvira! *Ven! Mira!* (Come! Look!)

42 ELVIRA: Filiberto, *qué pasó* (what happened)?

43 FILIBERTO: *Mira!*

44 ELVIRA: *Híjole!*

45 FILIBERTO: Beautiful, ripe *calabazas*.

46 ELVIRA: Ripe and beautiful! We can sell them at the *mercado* (market) and make so much money!

47 FILIBERTO: Where did they come from?

48 ELVIRA: What difference does it make? This is just the luck we've been waiting for.

49 FILIBERTO: Wait. We can't sell them.

50 ELVIRA: Can't sell them? *Estás loco*? (Are you crazy?)

51 FILIBERTO: We promised not to plant here.

52 ELVIRA: *Pues* (Well), if you're not selling them, I am. I'm going to load up the wagon with all of these beautiful, ripe *calabazas* and I'm not coming home until every last one is sold. If you want to try and peddle those sickly vegetables from the other garden, be my guest.

53 *(Filiberto looks at his puny vegetables, then at Elvira's beautiful* calabazas.*)*

54 FILIBERTO: Let's cut these and get them on the wagon!

55 ELVIRA: *Andale!* (Go for it!)

56 ACTOR 5: But as Filiberto and Elvira began to cut the *calabazas* from the vines, they made an incredible discovery. The squashes opened up when they touched them and inside—

57 FILIBERTO: Silver!

58 ELVIRA: Gold!

59 ACTOR 8: Every squash they opened **contained** a precious metal. Which of course to them meant—

60 ELVIRA & FILIBERTO: Money!!!

61 FILIBERTO: *(Extracting silver from a* calabaza:*)* Well this beats peddling bread on the streets!

62 ELVIRA: Ooooh. Let's spend it!

63 ACTOR 5: And spend, they did.

64 JOSIE: They didn't use the money to buy a new wagon.

65 JOSEFINA: Or to invest in new vegetable seeds for planting.

66 ACTOR 8: Or to purchase flour for Elvira's bread.

NOTES

Skill: Dramatic Elements and Structure

The short dialogue goes quickly back and forth between Filiberto and Elvira and lets me know this is a tense scene. I can see how stressed the two characters are by their problems.

The stage directions here help me understand what Filiberto is thinking. Since I'm reading and not watching the play, the stage directions let me know what is happening on stage. Filiberto is comparing his options, and the options are really unequal.

67 ACTOR 6: Instead, they bought new clothes, Elvira got some fine jewelry, and with the rest, they threw a party for all the neighbors.

68 *(Party music drops hard. Party with neighbors ensues.)*

69 ELVIRA: *Mira.* We had so much squash I made a delicious squash soup for the guests.

70 *(Party continues. GUESTS eat pumpkin soup and dance. Party dies down. Guests leave.)*

71 JOSIE: After the party, Filiberto and Elvira were cleaning up and . . .

72 *(Elvira pours soup into a container. The soup has turned to blood. She screams.)*

73 FILIBERTO: *Ay, Dios mío!* (Oh, my God!)

74 ELVIRA: What happened to my soup?

75 FILIBERTO: It's turned to blood!

76 ELVIRA: That can't be! There has to be some explanation.

77 FILIBERTO: *Sangre!* Blood! This is a *maldición* (curse)!

78 ELVIRA: *Cálmate!* (Calm down!)

79 FILIBERTO: We weren't supposed to plant in the west garden!

80 ELVIRA: Don't be **superstitious.**

81 FILIBERTO: We are not planting in that garden again. Ever!

82 ELVIRA: But, Filiberto—

83 FILIBERTO: It's a curse!!! *Ayyyy!*

84 *(Filiberto runs off terrified.)*

85 YOUNG JOSEFINA: So they went back to peddling bread and the sickly vegetables from the other garden.

86 ELVIRA: (*Peddling:*) *Pan caliente! Tengo pan caliente!* (Fresh bread! I have fresh bread here!)

87 FILIBERTO: *Zanahorias! Lechugas! Jitomate!* (Carrots! Lettuce! Tomato!)

88 *(Elvira and Filiberto at the end of the day counting their earnings.)*

89 ELVIRA: Ten, eleven, twelve, thirteen *centavos*. That's all!!!?

90 FILIBERTO: (*Sadly:*) That's all.

91 ELVIRA: We don't even have enough to make it through the week. Filiberto . . .

92 FILIBERTO: No.

93 ELVIRA: I'm tired of peddling bread on the streets and going to bed hungry. We're going to starve. Why shouldn't we have a little comfort and luxury?

94 FILIBERTO: But—

95 ELVIRA: Remember when we bought all those new clothes and threw a big party for all the neighbors? That was niiiiiice.

96 *(Filiberto regards her skeptically.)*

97 We're planting another crop of *calabazas* and this time we're planting more!

99 FILIBERTO: But, but, but—

99 ELVIRA: You say you aren't lucky? Hah! I say maybe this is the luck you've been waiting for. *Vámanos!* (Let's go!)

100 ACTOR 7: So Elvira and Filiberto sowed another crop in the garden. And yes, they planted even more.

101 ACTOR 6: The very next morning the garden was abundant with big, fat, ripe, healthy *calabazas*.

102 *(Elvira opens a squash and pulls out money.)*

103 ELVIRA: (*Gleefully:*) Ahhhh! I'm going to buy another new wardrobe! And this time we have enough money to **renovate** the house. Hey, we might even buy the land next door and expand!!!

104 JOSEFINA: And that's just what they did. They bought the land next door and built a brand new big house. They bought new furniture and then, because of course they wanted to share their new status with their neighbors, they threw a *fiesta*. A big *fiesta!*

NOTES

105 *(Party music drops again. Another party ensues. Elvira and Filiberto are greeted by guests as if they were royalty. And they love it.)*

106 YOUNG JOSEFINA: Elvira and Filiberto enjoyed the praise and considerable envy of their neighbors. Everyone drank and laughed and danced the night away. And then, just at the stroke of midnight, the heavens sent a moonbeam directly into the west garden.

107 GUEST 1: Hey everyone. Look! Look at those vines over there in the garden.

108 GUEST 2: Something's happening.

109 GUEST 1: They're growing!

110 GUEST 3: And . . . and they're moving this way!

111 GUEST 1: The vines are going to attack us!

112 GUEST 4: *Ay, Dios!* Everybody run!

113 *(Guests scramble. The music stops.)*

114 YOUNG JOSEFINA: The vines from the west garden had a life of their own. They ran along the ground, over the garden fences, around the patio and up the sides of the house until the whole place was engulfed in squash vines.

115 *(Guests cry out.)*

116 FILIBERTO: It's okay, everyone, just stay calm. There is an explanation for this, it's okay.

117 *(Elvira emerges from the crowd with squash vines growing out of her head.)*

118 ELVIRA: That's right, stay calm, stay calm.

119 *(Everyone freezes. They take in the horrible sight of Elvira.)*

120 GUEST 1: Aaaaaah!!!! Look at her hair!

121 GUEST 2: It's not hair!

122 GUEST 3: Vines are growing out of her skull!

123 GUEST 1: Aaaah! It's horrible.

124 GUEST 2: She's a—a—a monster!

125   GUEST 4: It's a curse!!

126   ELVIRA: Wait! What's wrong? Where is everybody going?

127   *(The guests scream and scramble away. Filiberto stands frozen.)*

128   What's happened?

129   FILIBERTO: You have . . . *enredaderas de calabaza* (pumpkin vines) growing
       out of your head.

130   ELVIRA: I . . . whaaaah?

131   *(Elvira feels her head.)*

132   Ahhhhhh!!!!!!!!! What's happened?

133   FILIBERTO: It's a *maldición*, I'm telling you! We never should have planted in
       that garden.

134   ELVIRA: Well, it's too late for that now.

135   FILIBERTO: What are we going to do?

136   ELVIRA: I'm going to tell you what *you're* going to do.

137   FILIBERTO: Me?!!

138   ELVIRA: You are going to find that Señor Trujillo from the card game, and get
       to the bottom of this.

139   FILIBERTO: Me . . . ?

140   ELVIRA: Do you expect me to do it? I can't go out in public like this. I'm a
       monster!

141   *(Elvira dissolves into tears.)*

142   FILIBERTO: Don't cry.

143   ELVIRA: I just wanted to have a few nice things for once. Does that make me
       a bad person?

144   FILIBERTO: Well, maybe we did overdo it a bit.

145   *(More tears from Elvira.)*

146 There, there. It's okay. I'll try to get to the bottom of this.

147 ELVIRA: Don't try. Do it!

148 JOSIE: Filiberto went door to door to see if he could locate someone from the Trujillo family.

149 FILIBERTO: Excuse me, do you know where I can find the Trujillos?

150 *(Sound of door shutting. He goes to next house.)*

151 Excuse me, do you know where I can find the Trujillos?

152 *(Sound of door shutting. He goes to next house.)*

153 ACTOR 6: Word had spread about a strange curse that had befallen Filiberto and his wife, and the town wanted nothing to do with them.

154 FILIBERTO: Excuse me, do you know who where I can find—

155 NEIGHBOR: You! We went to your lousy party and now everyone in town is allergic to squash! You're cursed! Get away from my house.

156 *(OLD MAN approaches. He's been following Filiberto.)*

157 OLD MAN: Hey. Psst. Psst. I know who you're looking for.

158 FILIBERTO: You do?

159 OLD MAN: Yes. And I'll tell you where to go under one condition.

160 FILIBERTO: What is it?

161 OLD MAN: Do you accept? Yes or no?

162 FILIBERTO: *(Tentatively:)* Yes.

163 OLD MAN: You must give *her* a message.

164 FILIBERTO: . . . *Bueno* (Okay), I can do that.

165 OLD MAN: Your land was previously owned by the *Tía* (Aunt). Eugenia Trujillo. Go to the house behind the big iron gates on the *Calle Aldama* (Aldama Street).

166 FILIBERTO: You mean . . . the house that everyone says is haunted?

167 OLD MAN: The very one. Do you want to find her or don't you?

168 FILIBERTO: I do. What's the message?

169 OLD MAN: Tell her . . . Rodolfo is still waiting for her.

170 FILIBERTO: Rodolfo is waiting.

171 OLD MAN: (*Correcting him:*) *Still* waiting.

172 FILIBERTO: Rodolfo is *still* waiting for her.

173 YOUNG JOSEFINA: Filiberto left the old man and set off to the stone house behind the big iron gates on the other side of town.

174 (*Filiberto clangs the iron knocker on the gate. Nothing. He clangs it again.*)

175 FILIBERTO: Hello! Is anybody home?

176 YOUNG JOSEFINA: He tried for hours. But no one answered.

177 (*He clangs again and calls out.*)

178 FILIBERTO: Is anybody home?

179 ACTOR 6: He became weary.

180 FILIBERTO: Anybody . . . ?

181 YOUNG JOSEFINA: And when he was ready to give up and walk away, he was reminded of poor Elvira waiting for him at home.

182 (*Memory of Elvira with vines growing out of her head.*)

183 ELVIRA: Don't try. Do it!!!

184 YOUNG JOSEFINA: So with no other options, Filiberto scaled the huge iron gate.

185 (*Filiberto climbs the tall gate and lands on the other side.*)

186 FILIBERTO: Such a magnificent courtyard. And grand fountain. Ooooh. I'm trespassing.

187 LA TÍA: (*Off:*) Who is there?

NOTES

188 FILIBERTO: Hello . . . Hello . . . My name is Filiberto. I'm sorry to enter your home. I knocked for hours but no one answered.

189 LA TÍA: (*Off.*) That means I don't want visitors, *tonto!*

190 FILIBERTO: I'm sorry, but errrr . . . I have a message for you.

191 LA TÍA: (*Off.*) A message?

192 FILIBERTO: Yes, but first . . . my wife and I live the home on *Calle San Antonio.* I won the land in . . .

193 (*A strange figure enters from the shadows. It's* LA TÍA *[The Aunt]. She is wearing black from head to toe and is covered in a diaphanous black veil.*)

194 LA TÍA: *Ah, si.* (Oh, yes.) My nephew told me you won the land fair and square. Now go, and stay away from us.

195 FILIBERTO: But . . . something strange is happening in the garden.

196 LA TÍA: Something strange?

197 FILIBERTO: Something horrible.

198 LA TÍA: Ah hah. You signed an agreement with the deed to that land.

199 FILIBERTO: Yes, but—

200 LA TÍA: Did you abide by that agreement?

201 FILIBERTO: Well, but my wife. Well . . . no. Not exactly—

202 LA TÍA: And now you've discovered the **consequences.**

203 FILIBERTO: Please. We have to sell the house back to you.

204 LA TÍA: Impossible.

205 FILIBERTO: We weren't told there was a curse. That wasn't fair.

206 LA TÍA: You signed the agreement!

207 FILIBERTO: But something has happened to my wife.

208 LA TÍA: Leave my home. You're trespassing.

209   FILIBERTO: We have nowhere else to turn.

210   LA TÍA: You made your choice and sealed your fate. Now, get out!

211   *(She turns to leave.)*

212   FILIBERTO: Wait, please!

213   *(Filiberto pursues, reaches out and grabs her veil. He unwittingly pulls it off her head, revealing an elaborate spray of squash vines coming out of her skull. She screams.)*

214   LA TÍA: Don't look at me!

215   FILIBERTO: You too!

216   LA TÍA: Leave me alone.

217   FILIBERTO: What causes this? Is it a *maldición?*

218   LA TÍA: Yes! Yes! Yes! What else?

219   FILIBERTO: We have to undo what's been done.

220   LA TÍA: You can't.

221   FILIBERTO: There has to be a way.

222   LA TÍA: You aren't brave enough to face it. No one is. I chose to live my life like this instead.

223   FILIBERTO: But . . . I'll face it. I have to.

224   LA TÍA: *(Sizing him up:)* You? Bah!

225   FILIBERTO: Wha . . . what is it? Tell me, please. I have to help my wife!

226   LA TÍA: Dig into the dirt in the west garden at midnight on a full moon. And if you attempt it, heaven help you.

227   FILIBERTO: Why? What's there?

228   LA TÍA: No one knows. For centuries no one has been brave enough or foolish enough to try.

229   FILIBERTO: I will.

NOTES

230   LA TÍA: Hmph!

231   FILIBERTO: For my wife, I will be brave!

232   *(He starts to leave. She calls after him.)*

233   LA TÍA: And my message?

234   FILIBERTO: Ah. Your message. The message is—Rodolfo is still waiting for you.

235   LA TÍA: *(A painful memory:)* Rodolfo . . . ?

236   *(La Tía begins to cry. She covers her head with the veil as she runs off sobbing. Filiberto heads home.)*

237   JOSIE: As fate would have it, that very night there was a full moon and by the time Filiberto returned home, it was just about midnight . . .

238   *(Someone hands Filiberto a shovel. He begins digging. Elvira enters.)*

239   ELVIRA: Filiberto, I was so worried about you. What are you doing?

240   FILIBERTO: I found the woman who owned this place.

241   ELVIRA: And? Will she buy it back from us?

242   FILIBERTO: No, but she told me what has to be done.

243   ELVIRA: That's why you're digging?

244   FILIBERTO: There's no telling what kind of evil is beneath this soil. It might be the devil himself. But I'm going to do it and break this curse.

245   ELVIRA: But Filiberto.

246   FILIBERTO: Go back to the house and wait for me. Please. Just go.

247   ELVIRA: Whatever evils there are to face, we'll face them together.

248   *(Someone hands Elvira a shovel. They dig.)*

249   YOUNG JOSEFINA: So together, they dug. Filiberto told Elvira about the old *Tía* and the old man, and he told her about the message from Rodolfo. And they dug all through the night under the full moon. Until—

250   *(Filiberto's shovel hits a hard surface.)*

251 FILIBERTO: Here! I've found something.

252 *(Elvira moves to Filiberto and together they uncover his discovery.)*

253 ELVIRA: What is this?

254 FILIBERTO: It's a huge wooden box, like a . . .

255 FILIBERTO & ELVIRA: *(Recoiling in fear:)* . . . A coffin!

256 ELVIRA: Don't go near it. Maybe it's my fate to live the rest of my life as this horrible thing. Maybe I deserve this for being so greedy.

257 FILIBERTO: We have to free you. And who knows how many generations of people fell into this maldición. It has to stop.

258 *(Filiberto reaches down to open the coffin.)*

259 ELVIRA: Wait! What if this is a trick?

260 FILIBERTO: We have to take that chance.

261 ELVIRA: Wait! What if the old woman is part of all this evil?

262 FILIBERTO: There's no way to know. Stand back!

263 ELVIRA: Filiberto!!!

264 *(Filiberto opens the coffin. They gasp.)*

265 FILIBERTO: *Un esqueleto!* (A skeleton!)

266 ELVIRA: And look! Gold! Silver!

267 FILIBERTO: It's a fortune!

268 ELVIRA: And jewels! Oooh, they're so beautiful!

269 FILIBERTO: Don't touch them!

270 ELVIRA: But they're so shiny and pretty!

271 *(She grabs at the jewels. Music swells as a huge ESQUELETO [skeleton] emerges from the coffin, along with glittering silver and gold pieces. Filiberto and Elvira scream. The skeleton towers over them.)*

272   EL ESQUELETO: Who are you?

273   FILIBERTO: We are Filiberto and Elvira. We live here on this land.

274   EL ESQUELETO: And why do you open my coffin?

275   ELVIRA: There's been a *maldición*.

276   EL ESQUELETO: What kind of *maldición*?

277   ELVIRA: What kind? Hellooooo??? Look at me!

278   FILIBERTO: We were told if we find the secret buried in this garden, we could cure the *maldición*.

279   EL ESQUELETO: The *maldición* of this garden is against greed. Now the story is revealed. When I, Juan Ortiz Orizaba, died, my treasure was buried with me to hide it from the greedy Spaniards. But before my wife could dig the treasure out, death took her and I've been stuck here ever since. Look into the coffin.

280   *(Filiberto and Elvira peer into the coffin.)*

281   FILIBERTO: Gold and silver!

282   ELVIRA: And jewels!

283   EL ESQUELETO: The *maldición* ends when there is no more greed on this land or in this house!

284   ELVIRA: No more greed.

285   FILIBERTO: We promise!

286   ELVIRA: Er . . . okay!

287   EL ESQUELETO: Riches are for the purpose of generosity!

288   FILIBERTO: *La generosidad* (generosity)!

289   *(A huge wind kicks up. It swirls around Filiberto and Elvira. El Esqueleto disappears. Suddenly Elvira is back to normal.)*

290   FILIBERTO: Your head!

291   ELVIRA: *(Feeling her head:)* I'm me again!

NOTES

292   *(They embrace.* La Tía *enters. She no longer has vines growing out of her skull.)*

293   LA TÍA: You did it. You had the courage to remove the curse.

294   FILIBERTO: (*Reaching to Elvira:*) We did it, together.

295   *(The Old Man enters.)*

296   LA TÍA: Rodolfo.

297   OLD MAN: I heard a great wind and saw a bright light coming from this place of my fondest memories.

298   LA TÍA: You came back.

299   OLD MAN: I told you I would wait for you.

300   LA TÍA: I'm sorry I shunned you, but I couldn't bear for you to look at me, I was so horrible.

301   OLD MAN: And I told you it didn't matter, *mi amor.*

302   (La Tía *and the Old Man embrace.)*

303   FILIBERTO: And now we will share in these riches . . . with others!

304   LA TÍA: What a good idea. We can build a library for the town.

305   ELVIRA: And start an orphanage.

306   FILIBERTO: And a public garden so people can plant vegetables for their families.

307   OLD MAN: There are many uses for these treasures!

308   ELVIRA: (*To audience:*) Filiberto and Elvira found many ways to give to others. They went down in the history of the *pueblo* as great philanthropists.

309   FILIBERTO: (*To audience:*) But neither of them ever went near a squash again.

310   *(Music rises. Actors take a bow, then quickly take their places for the next tale. Young Josefina steps down.)*

Please note that excerpts and passages in the StudySync® library and this workbook are intended as touchstones to generate interest in an author's work. The excerpts and passages do not substitute for the reading of entire texts, and StudySync® strongly recommends that students seek out and purchase the whole literary or informational work in order to experience it as the author intended. Links to online resellers are available in our digital library. In addition, complete works may be ordered through an authorized reseller by filling out and returning to StudySync® the order form enclosed in this workbook.

Reading & Writing Companion   **119**

First Read

Read *Cuentos de Josefina*. After you read, complete the Think Questions below.

 THINK QUESTIONS

1. Why do you think Filiberto remarks, "Maybe I wasn't born under a lucky star after all"? Explain.

2. Although bad things keep happening to them, Filiberto and Elvira continue to plant crops in the west garden. Why? Explain, citing specific evidence from the text.

3. How do Filiberto and Elvira gain perspective or wisdom from their struggles? Cite textual evidence to support your answer.

4. Read the following dictionary entry:

   contain
   con•tain \ kən'tān \ verb
   1. to carry or hold something within
   2. to control or restrain a feeling
   3. to stop something from spreading further

   Which definition most closely matches the meaning of **contain** as it is used in the text? Write the correct definition of *contain* here and explain how you figured out the correct meaning.

5. Based on context clues in the text, what do you think **consequences** means as it is used in paragraph 202? Write your best definition of *consequences* here, explaining how you arrived at its meaning. Does this word have a positive, negative, or neutral connotation?

Skill: Dramatic Elements and Structure

Use the Checklist to analyze Dramatic Elements and Structure in *Cuentos de Josefina*. Refer to the sample student annotations about Dramatic Elements and Structure in the text.

••• CHECKLIST FOR DRAMATIC ELEMENTS AND STRUCTURE

In order to identify the dramatic elements and structure of a drama, note the following:

✓ the form of the drama, such as comedy or tragedy

✓ how the acts and scenes advance the plot

✓ the setting of the play and whether or how it changes in each act or scene

✓ the language of the play, such as prose or verse, as spoken by characters

✓ the use of dramatic devices such as

- soliloquy, when a character speaks his or her thoughts aloud directly to the audience while alone on stage

- asides, when a character shares private thoughts with the audience when other characters are on stage

- the information in stage directions, including lighting, sound, and set, as well as details about characters, including exits and entrances

To analyze how a drama's form or structure contributes to its meaning, consider the following questions:

✓ How does the use of figurative language contribute to the play's meaning?

✓ How is each act or scene structured? How do characters enter and leave, how do they speak to each other, and what happens as a result?

✓ How does the form, such as verse, contribute to the theme or message?

Please note that excerpts and passages in the StudySync® library and this workbook are intended as touchstones to generate interest in an author's work. The excerpts and passages do not substitute for the reading of entire texts, and StudySync® strongly recommends that students seek out and purchase the whole literary or informational work in order to experience it as the author intended. Links to online resellers are available in our digital library. In addition, complete works may be ordered through an authorized reseller by filling out and returning to StudySync® the order form enclosed in this workbook.

Reading & Writing Companion

121

Skill: Dramatic Elements and Structure

Reread paragraphs 178–193 of *Cuentos de Josefina*. Then, using the Checklist on the previous page, answer the multiple-choice questions below.

⟳ YOUR TURN

1. This question has two parts. First, answer Part A. Then, answer Part B.

   Part A What is the effect of the stage directions on this scene?

   ○ A. The stage directions help the reader picture what is happening on stage.
   ○ B. The stage directions help the reader understand what the characters are thinking.
   ○ C. The stage directions help the reader figure out what will happen next in the plot.
   ○ D. The stage directions help the reader identify the villain and the hero of the story.

   Part B Which of the following details BEST supports your response to Part A?

   ○ A. He became weary.
   ○ B. (Filiberto climbs the tall gate and lands on the other side.)
   ○ C. I'm sorry to enter your home. I knocked for hours but no one answered.
   ○ D. Filiberto scaled the huge iron gate.

CUENTOS DE JOSEFINA
(JOSEPHINE'S TALES)

Close Read

Reread *Cuentos de Josefina.* As you reread, complete the Skills Focus questions below. Then use your answers and annotations from the questions to help you complete the Write activity.

◎ SKILLS FOCUS

1. Identify evidence of how the playwright uses stage directions or dialogue to portray the characters. Explain what the dramatic elements tell you about the characters and why they choose to act as they do.

2. Identify details that reveal the qualities of the characters and setting in the play. Explain how the characters and setting influence the events of the plot of the play.

3. How do the narrators' asides influence the plot and tone of the play? Explain the dramatic element and how it influences your understanding of the play.

4. Identify examples that state or imply one or more universal themes in the play. Explain how the theme is reflected in the characters' actions and in the development of the plot.

5. Identify evidence of how Filiberto and Elvira stood out from the crowd, in both negative and positive ways. Explain how their desire to stand out from, or blend in with, the crowd drives the plot of the drama.

✏ WRITE

LITERARY ANALYSIS: Folktales have wide and lasting appeal because they teach lessons about universal ideas and experiences common across cultures and time periods. Write a response in which you identify a lesson with a universal appeal. In your response, explain how the author uses dramatic elements and structures, such as dialogue and asides, to help teach a lesson or moral.

Please note that excerpts and passages in the StudySync® library and this workbook are intended as touchstones to generate interest in an author's work. The excerpts and passages do not substitute for the reading of entire texts, and StudySync® strongly recommends that students seek out and purchase the whole literary or informational work in order to experience it as the author intended. Links to online resellers are available in our digital library. In addition, complete works may be ordered through an authorized reseller by filling out and returning to StudySync® the order form enclosed in this workbook.

Reading & Writing Companion **123**

Extended
Oral
Project and
Grammar

EXTENDED
ORAL
PROJECT

ORAL
PRESENTATION
PROCESS
PLAN

Oral Presentation Process: Plan

| PLAN | DRAFT | REVISE | EDIT AND PRESENT |

The texts in *The Power of One* unit take a variety of forms. Some of them are intended to be performed on a stage, and some are meant to be read on the page. You have also read, listened to, or watched a long list of powerful stories, plays, and other works throughout the year. We can reflect on which texts or productions best educate, entertain, and inspire audiences. We can also think about and research why these works are important and what message their authors have about individuals and society.

WRITING PROMPT

What literary work, film, or dramatic production would you recommend to your classmates? Why is this work important? How does this work entertain, inspire, or educate?

Prepare an argumentative presentation convincing your classmates to read or see a favorite literary work, film, or dramatic production. Be sure to include a clear position or thesis statement. In your reasoning, explain why this work is important and what made it entertaining, educational, or inspirational. Include evidence from at least three reliable sources. One source should be your recommended work itself and one should include diverse media formats, including video, audio, graphics, and print or digital texts. Research focuses could include the work's deeper message, historical or cultural significance, or genre or information about the author or director.

In your presentation, be sure to employ the following in order to communicate your ideas effectively:

- a clear position or thesis statement
- reasons and evidence that support the position
- reliable and credible sources
- consistent eye contact and clear oral communication
- gestures to emphasize or communicate ideas visually
- multimedia and visual displays
- a works cited page

Introduction to Oral Presentation

Argumentative oral presentations use body language, visual supports, and engaging writing to convince an audience about an issue. Good oral presentations use effective speaking techniques, relevant facts and anecdotes, and a purposeful structure. The characteristics of argumentative oral presentations include:

- a clear position or thesis statement

- reasons and evidence that support the position

- reliable and credible sources

- consistent eye contact and clear oral communication

- gestures to emphasize or communicate ideas visually

- multimedia and visual displays

- a works cited page

These characteristics can be organized into four major categories: context, structure, style and language, and elements of effective communication. As you continue with this Extended Oral Project, you'll receive more instruction and practice in crafting each of the presentation characteristics to create your oral presentation.

Before you get started on your own argumentative oral presentation, read this oral presentation that one student, Theo, wrote in response to the writing prompt. As you read the Model, highlight and annotate the features of argumentative writing that Theo included in his oral presentation.

☰ STUDENT MODEL

NOTES

Monsters and a Message

By Theo

Introduction:

When you look at this picture of some neighbors, you might think they look concerned. Maybe they are discussing the guy who never cuts his grass. You would never know that chaos is about to break out on Maple Street. If you're like me, when you see a black-and-white TV show, you immediately assume that it is going to be boring and old-fashioned.

Introduction (Continued):

But I think it's worth taking a chance on an episode of *The Twilight Zone* series called "The Monsters Are Due on Maple Street." Even though the episode aired in 1960, it tells an important story.

Position or Thesis Statement:

I recommend "The Monsters Are Due on Maple Street" for three reasons.

- First, it's entertaining to watch because it has elements of science fiction and suspense.

- Second, it comments on important historical and political issues of its time.

- Finally, the episode teaches a valuable lesson about the danger of spreading rumors.

I recommend "The Monsters Are Due on Maple Street" because...

- It is entertaining to watch because it has elements of science fiction and suspense.
- It comments on important historical and political issues of its time.
- The episode teaches a valuable lesson about the danger of spreading rumors.

Reason #1:

The science-fiction elements and suspense in "The Monsters Are Due on Maple Street" keep the audience guessing and on the edge of their seat. Science fiction is a genre that often tells stories about futuristic science and technology, outer space, or aliens. Suspense is a genre that heightens feelings of surprise, excitement, and anxiety. The episode has elements of science fiction and ends in a twist. The viewers have to keep asking themselves whether things are coincidences or evidence of something the neighbors are trying to hide.

Entertaining Science Fiction and Suspense Elements

Science Fiction
- Often tells stories about futuristic science and technology, outer space, or aliens
- Deals with the impact of actual or imagined science on society or individual people

Suspense
- Gives readers or viewers feelings of surprise, excitement, or anxiety
- Creates tension by putting the characters in a fast-paced and interesting story that ends with a twist

Reason #1 (Continued):

First, a strange object passes over the town, causing electronics to stop working. Then, Les Goodman's car starts on its own, and people become suspicious, thinking he might be part of an alien invasion. Goodman struggles to explain what is happening to him. He says, "So I've got a car that starts by itself . . . I don't know why the car works—it just does!" Neither the characters nor the viewers know what to believe. Is it aliens? Is it something else? Nobody knows.

Reason #1 (Continued):

"The Monsters Are Due on Maple Street" also grabs your attention through tense and suspenseful action. From the moment the object passes over Maple Street, you begin to feel as though something is not right. Goodman is frightened, too. His dialogue foreshadows the violence to come. He says, "As God is my witness . . . you're letting something begin here that's a nightmare!" Knowing that something bad might happen makes you want to watch every scene closely. The episode's plot is full of surprises that will make your jaw drop and your heart pound in your chest. You never know what is going to happen next.

Please note that excerpts and passages in the StudySync® library and this workbook are intended as touchstones to generate interest in an author's work. The excerpts and passages do not substitute for the reading of entire texts, and StudySync® strongly recommends that students seek out and purchase the whole literary or informational work in order to experience it as the author intended. Links to online resellers are available in our digital library. In addition, complete works may be ordered through an authorized reseller by filling out and returning to StudySync® the order form enclosed in this workbook.

Reading & Writing Companion   129

NOTES

Reason #2:

Many episodes of *The Twilight Zone*, including "The Monsters Are Due on Maple Street," also addressed important historical and political issues of the time. Rod Serling could educate and inform people on historical or political issues using science fiction.

Commentary on Important Politics and History

"I found that it was all right to have Martians saying things that Democrats and Republicans could never say."
-Rod Serling, creator of *The Twilight Zone*

"Rod Serling: Submitted for Your Approval" (1995)

Reason #2 (Continued):

"The Monsters Are Due on Maple Street" was written in 1960, just years after the Red Scare. The Red Scare was a time in American history when many people were fearful of communist politics. During the Red Scare, many people were spying on neighbors to uncover secret communists. Some people were arrested. "Reds" was a nickname for communists at the time. Serling created "The Monsters Are Due on Maple Street" in response to a rising distrust between

Copyright © BookheadEd Learning, LLC

some Americans. The actions of the neighbors on Maple Street can be seen as commentary on the paranoia associated with the Red Scare. However, this episode wasn't just entertainment or a history lesson; it's also a life lesson.

Reason #3:

The story also sends a powerful message about gossip. It reminds audiences that spreading unfair rumors can lead to disaster.

NOTES

Reason #3 (Continued):

In the episode, enough people spread the rumor that Goodman is dangerous that everyone begins to think it is true. Another neighbor, Steve, tries to convince people to fight back against group pressure. He promises that "the only thing that's gonna happen is that we'll eat each other up alive." Steve has the courage to stand up for Goodman even though everyone is spreading bad rumors about him. Steve does not want to accuse someone who could be innocent.

An Important Lesson About Gossip

"You're standing here all set to crucify—all set to find a scapegoat—all desperate to point some kind of finger at a neighbor! Well now look, friends, the only thing that's gonna happen is that we'll eat each other up alive—"

"The Monsters Are Due on Maple Street" (1960)

Reason #3 (Continued):

Unfortunately, Steve's warning is too late. At the episode's climax, a man named Charlie shoots and kills a shadowy figure that he thinks is a monster. The "monster" turns out to be their neighbor, Pete Van Horn. Afterwards, Charlie is frightened, and he asks, "How was I supposed to know he wasn't a monster or something?" So many people had shared the rumor of a monster that Charlie thought the monster had to be real. If there had not been a terrible rumor, Charlie probably would not have acted so violently.

"How was I supposed to know he wasn't a monster or something? We're all scared of the same thing, I was just tryin' to . . . trying' to protect my home, that's all! Look, all of you, that's all I was tryin' to do."

"The Monsters Are Due on Maple Street" (1960)

Conclusion:

"The Monsters Are Due on Maple Street" is much more than an exciting *Twilight Zone* episode. It uses suspense and attention-grabbing science-fiction elements. You will enjoy a gripping story while learning a bit about the political and historical topics of the 1950s and '60s. You also learn a lesson that applies just as well to rumors and gossip as it does to aliens.

Thank You and Works Cited:

Thank you for your time, and I hope you watch Rod Serling's "The Monsters Are Due on Maple Street" soon!

Works Cited

"Joseph McCarthy Begins Hearings Investigating U.S. Army." *History.com*, A&E Television Networks, 13 Nov. 2009, https://www.history.com/this-day-in-history/mccarthy-army-hearings-begin.

NBC News. "The Headline for a Newspaper Reads, 'All 11 Reds Are Convicted.'" *NBC News Archives Xpress*, https://www.nbcnewsarchivesxpress.com/contentdetails/6921.

"Rod Serling: Submitted for Your Approval." *American Masters*, season 10, episode 1, PBS, 29 Nov. 1995.

"The Monsters Are Due on Maple Street." *The Twilight Zone*, season 1, episode 22, CBS, 4 Mar. 1960.

"Top 10 Twilight Zone Episodes." *Time*, 2 Oct. 2009, http://entertainment.time.com/2009/10/02/top-10-twilight-zone-episodes/slide/the-monsters-are-due-on-maple-street-1960/.

Please note that excerpts and passages in the StudySync® library and this workbook are intended as touchstones to generate interest in an author's work. The excerpts and passages do not substitute for the reading of entire texts, and StudySync® strongly recommends that students seek out and purchase the whole literary or informational work in order to experience it as the author intended. Links to online resellers are available in our digital library. In addition, complete works may be ordered through an authorized reseller by filling out and returning to StudySync® the order form enclosed in this workbook.

Reading & Writing Companion

133

WRITE

Writers often take notes about arguments before they sit down to write. Think about what you've learned so far about organizing argumentative presentations to help you begin prewriting.

- **Purpose:** What literary work, film, or dramatic production have you enjoyed this year? Why should your classmates watch or read this work?

- **Reasons:** Why is this work important? How does this work entertain, inspire, or educate?

- **Evidence:** What evidence and details from your literary work, film, or dramatic production will you include? What other research might you need to do about the author or director, the genre, or the work's historical or cultural importance?

- **Organization:** How can you organize your presentation so that it is clear and easy to follow?

- **Clear Communication:** Who is your audience? How will you make sure that your audience can hear and understand you?

- **Technology and Visual Aids:** How can you use technology to engage your audience? What images or other visual aids could you use during your presentation?

Response Instructions

Use the questions in the bulleted list to write a one-paragraph summary. Your summary should describe what you will discuss in your oral presentation like the one on the previous pages.

Don't worry about including all of the details now; focus only on the most essential and important elements. You will refer back to this short summary as you continue through the steps of the writing process.

Skill: Evaluating Sources

••• CHECKLIST FOR EVALUATING SOURCES

First, reread the sources you gathered and identify the following:

- what kind of source it is, including video, audio, or text, and where the source comes from

- where information seems inaccurate, biased, or outdated

- where information seems irrelevant or incomplete

In order to use advanced searches to gather relevant, credible, and accurate print and digital sources, use the following questions as a guide:

- Is the material published by a well-established source or expert author?

- Is the material up-to-date or based on the most current information?

- Is the material factual, and can it be verified by another source?

- Are there specific terms or phrases in my research question that I can use to adjust my search?

- Can I use "and," "or," or "not" to expand or limit my search?

- Can I use quotation marks to search for exact phrases?

Please note that excerpts and passages in the StudySync® library and this workbook are intended as touchstones to generate interest in an author's work. The excerpts and passages do not substitute for the reading of entire texts, and StudySync® strongly recommends that students seek out and purchase the whole literary or informational work in order to experience it as the author intended. Links to online resellers are available in our digital library. In addition, complete works may be ordered through an authorized reseller by filling out and returning to StudySync® the order form enclosed in this workbook.

Reading & Writing
Companion

135

⟳ YOUR TURN

Read the factors below. Then, complete the chart by placing them into two categories: those that show a source is credible and reliable and those that do not.

	Factors
A	The video is objective, uses clear facts, and includes several different viewpoints.
B	The author is a reporter for an internationally recognized newspaper.
C	The article states only the author's first name and does not include any expert qualifications.
D	The text relies on loaded language or broad generalizations to persuade readers.
E	The article includes clear arguments and counterarguments that can be verified by other sources.
F	The website is for a personal podcast.

Credible and Reliable	Not Credible or Reliable

YOUR TURN

Complete the chart below by filling in the title and author of a source and answering the questions about it.

Source Title and Author:	
Reliable: Is the source material up-to-date or based on the most current information?	
Credible: Is the material published by a well-established source or expert author?	
Accurate: Is the material factual, and can it be verified by another source?	
Evaluation: Should I use this source in my oral presentation?	

Please note that excerpts and passages in the StudySync® library and this workbook are intended as touchstones to generate interest in an author's work. The excerpts and passages do not substitute for the reading of entire texts, and StudySync® strongly recommends that students seek out and purchase the whole literary or informational work in order to experience it as the author intended. Links to online resellers are available in our digital library. In addition, complete works may be ordered through an authorized reseller by filling out and returning to StudySync® the order form enclosed in this workbook.

Reading & Writing Companion   **137**

Skill: Organizing an Oral Presentation

In order to present claims and findings using appropriate eye contact, adequate volume, and clear pronunciation, do the following:

- Decide whether your presentation will be delivered to entertain, critique, inform, or persuade.

- Identify your audience in order to create your content.

- Choose a style for your oral presentation, either formal or informal.

- Use pertinent, or relative and appropriate, descriptions, facts, and details.

- Emphasize salient, or relevant and significant, points in a focused, clear manner.

- Include multimedia components and visual displays to clarify claims and findings and emphasize salient, or relevant, points.

- Use appropriate eye contact, adequate volume, and clear pronunciation.

To present claims and findings using appropriate eye contact, adequate volume, and clear pronunciation, consider the following questions:

- Have I decided on the purpose of my presentation and identified my audience?

- Have I chosen a style for my oral presentation, either formal or informal?

- Did I make sure that the descriptions, facts, and details I present are pertinent and support what I have to say?

- Have I emphasized relevant, salient points in a clear, coherent manner?

- Did I include multimedia components and visual displays to clarify claims and emphasize salient points?

- Did I practice using appropriate eye contact, adequate volume, and clear pronunciation?

↻ YOUR TURN

Read the following quotations from a student's outline of her oral presentation and complete the chart on the next page by matching each with the corresponding component of her oral presentation.

	Quotations
A	My classmates and my teachers.
B	Finally, the most important reason to read it is because even though it is an old story, readers today can still relate to the theme and message about greed.
C	I think everyone should read "The Tale of the Haunted Squash" because it is entertaining, teaches a lesson about greed, and reminds readers to be grateful.
D	I also need to make eye contact with audience members in different parts of the room as I speak.
E	I will use a formal style because this is an academic presentation to my peers and teachers.
F	I will repeat my evaluation, reminding readers that this story will entertain them and teach them a lesson about greed. Then I will include a works cited slide to make sure I properly credit all my sources.
G	This is a funny and entertaining story; readers will laugh at the characters and their mishaps throughout the play.
H	I will include pictures of squash and a garden. I might try to find a video clip of the play or an audio clip of the story being told in the original Spanish.
I	To convince my classmates that they should read "The Tale of the Haunted Squash."
J	Although this story is filled with humor, it also has exciting and dramatic moments that will keep readers on the edge of their seats as they read.

YOUR TURN

Oral Presentation Component	Quotation from Oral Presentation Outline
Purpose	
Audience	
Style	
Thesis Statement	
Reason 1	
Reason 2	
Reason 3	
Conclusion	
Multimedia	
Oral Presentation Skills	

WRITE

Use the questions in the checklist to outline your oral presentation. Be sure to present your thesis and support for that thesis in a logical order. Your outline should emphasize important points and show how they are connected to one another.

Skill: Considering Audience and Purpose

In order to adapt speech to a variety of contexts and tasks, demonstrating a command of formal English when indicated or appropriate, note the following:

- your claims, findings, or salient points as well as pertinent facts, details, or examples

- your purpose, or reason for presenting

- your audience, the people who listen to an oral response or presentation

- your register, including your use of formal or informal English

- your volume and pronunciation of words

- your tone, or your attitude toward your subject matter

- your vocabulary and voice, including words to use for a specific occasion or in a particular context

To better understand how to adapt speech to a variety of contexts and tasks, demonstrating a command of formal English when indicated or appropriate, consider the following questions:

- What are my claims or findings? How can I emphasize my salient points?

- Did I include pertinent facts, details, or examples to support my claims or points in my presentation?

- What is my purpose for my oral response or presentation?

- Who is listening to my oral response or presentation?

- How should I adapt or change my register for my audience and task?

- What volume should I use? Do I know how to pronounce all the words correctly?

- How should I change my voice, tone, or vocabulary?

YOUR TURN

Read each example of student behaviors during a presentation. Then, complete the chart by filling in the strategy that best matches each example.

Strategies			
Vocabulary	Voice	Tone	Register

Example	Strategy
A student speaks loudly and lively to show that she finds the topic of her presentation exciting.	
A student uses words like *electorate* and *house of representatives* to prove her expertise in politics to the audience.	
A student makes jokes to emphasize his friendly personality and the humor in his presentation topic.	
A student uses slang because he is talking to a small group of his friends.	

✎ WRITE

Form a small group with a few of your classmates. Take turns explaining the ideas in your outline to the group. When you finish, write a reflection about your purpose and your interaction with the audience. What was your purpose for speaking? How did your audience affect how you spoke? How did you use register, tone, and voice to accomplish your purpose and reach your audience? What vocabulary words or sentences will you change when writing your draft to better adapt your speech and emphasize your points?

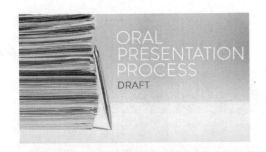

Oral Presentation Process: Draft

PLAN	DRAFT	REVISE	EDIT AND PRESENT

You have already made progress toward writing your oral presentation. Now it is time to draft your argumentative oral presentation.

✎ WRITE

Use your plan and other responses in your Binder to draft your oral presentation. You may also have new ideas as you begin drafting. Feel free to explore those new ideas as you have them. You can also ask yourself these questions:

- Have I clearly stated a position about a literary work, film, or production?
- Do I give logical reasons in my critique of the literary work, film, or production?
- Have I organized my ideas using a clear text structure?

Before you submit your draft, read it over carefully. You want to be sure that you've responded to all aspects of the prompt.

Here is Theo's oral presentation draft. As you read, notice how Theo develops his draft to grab the audience's attention.

NOTES

Skill:
Communicating Ideas

Theo adds important information so his readers will understand whom or what he is discussing.

Skill:
Reasons and Relevant Evidence

Theo's presentation includes information that is not sufficiently supported by evidence and sound reasoning. He did not provide enough evidence to support his claim. Theo decides to revise his focus on a single claim and add details that help explain his ideas.

☰ STUDENT MODEL: FIRST DRAFT

Monsters and a Message

When you look at this picture of some neighbors, you might think they look concerned, so you would never know that chaos is about to breakout on Maple Street. [slide with neighbors talking and looking]. If you're like me, you see a black-and-white TV show and immediately assume that it is going to be boring and old-fashioned. ~~But I think it's worth taking a chance on "The Monsters Are Due on Maple Street".~~

But I think it's worth taking a chance on an episode of *The Twilight Zone* series called "The Monsters Are Due on Maple Street."

It's entertaining to watch and you can actually learn a lot about history from this episode and learn an important lesson for today. I recommend "The Monsters Are Due on Maple Street" because the episode tells an important story.

The episode is entertaining because the science-fiction and suspense elements. A bunch of weird things happen in the episode. The viewers have to keep asking themselves whether things are coincidences. Goodman is frightened. His dialog foreshadows the violence in the episode. He says, "As God is my witness . . . you're letting something begin here that's a nightmare!" ~~Knowing that something bad might happen makes you want to watch every scene closely. You want to know what is going to happen next!~~

Knowing that something bad might happen makes you want to watch every scene closely. The episode's plot is full of surprises that will make your jaw drop and your heart pound in your chest. You never know what is going to happen next.

Many episodes of *The Twilight Zone* including "The Monsters Are Due on Maple Street" addressed important social and political issues of the time. Rod Serling could educate and inform people on social or political issues using science fiction. He once said, "I found it was all right to have Martians saying things Democrats or Republicans could never say" (PBS American Masters).

Skill: Sources and Citations

[Show slide with quote.]

"I found that it was all right to have Martians saying things that Democrats and Republicans could never say."

–Rod Serling, creator of *The Twilight Zone*

"Rod Serling: Submitted for Your Approval" (1995)

"The Monsters Are Due on Maple Street" was written in 1960, just years before The Red Scare [slide with information about the Red Scare or video]. The Red Scare was a time in American history when people were fearful of communist politics, "Reds" was a nickname for communists during this time. During the Red Scare, many neighbors were spying on neighbors to uncover secret communists. Some people were even arrested. Serling created "The Monsters Are Due on Maple Street" in response to rise in distrust between Americans.

"The Monsters Are Due on Maple Street" reminds audiences that spreading unfair rumors can lead to disaster. In the episode, enough people spread the rumor that Goodman is dangerous that everyone begins to think it is true. A man tries to convince people to fight back against group pressure. It promises that "the only thing that's gonna happen is that we'll eat each other up alive" [slide with this quote]. The man has the courage to stand up for Goodman even though everyone is spreading bad rumors about the man. Steve does not want to hurt someone who is actually innocent. Unfortunately, his warning is too late. At the episode's climax, a man named Charlie shoots and kills a shadowy figure. Charlie thinks the figure is a monster. Charlie eventually figures out the the "monster" is his neighbor, Pete Van Horn. Charlie is frightened, and he asks, "How was I supposed to know he wasn't a monster or something?" Charlie thought the monster had to be real because so many people had shared the rumor of a monster. If there had not been a terrible rumor, Charlie probably would not have acted so violently.

"The Monsters Are Due on Maple Street" is much more than an exciting TV episode. Watching the episode, you question what is real, and you wonder what will happen next. I recommend that everyone watch this episode to enjoy a gripping story and to learn more about the politics of the 1950s and 60s. You will also learn a lesson that applies just as well to rumors and gossip as it does to aliens! [slide with thank you to the audience and my works cited page after]

NOTES

The quotation on Theo's slide credits the speaker, as well as the title of the source in which Theo found the quote. Theo also made sure to include the publication date. Although simply identifying the title of the work would have been enough to connect the quote to the corresponding entry in the works cited list, the additional reference to the date lends credibility to his presentation.

Skill:
Communicating Ideas

••• CHECKLIST FOR COMMUNICATING IDEAS

In order to present claims and findings using appropriate eye contact, adequate volume, and clear pronunciation, note the following:

- When writing your presentation, emphasize salient, or relevant and significant, points.

- Present your claims and findings in a focused, coherent way, making sure that the information you present is organized clearly and easily understandable.

- Use pertinent, or valid and important, facts and details to support and accentuate, or highlight, the main ideas or themes in your presentation.

- Include examples wherever possible to support your main idea.

- Remember to use adequate eye contact.

- Speak at an adequate volume so you can be heard by everyone.

- Use correct pronunciation.

To better understand how to present claims and findings and use appropriate eye contact, adequate volume, and clear pronunciation, consider the following questions:

- Have I used appropriate eye contact when giving my presentation?

- Did I speak at an adequate volume and use correct pronunciation?

- Did I include pertinent facts and details and accentuate the main ideas or themes in my presentation?

- Were my findings presented in a clear and coherent way?

↻ YOUR TURN

Below are several examples of students communicating their ideas. To complete the chart, fill in the strategy that matches each example.

Strategies
Keep your posture
Make eye contact
Speak clearly
Use gestures

Example	Strategy
A student slows down her speech while pronouncing words in a foreign language.	
A student practices how he will stand to make sure he will be comfortable throughout his presentation.	
A student uses her fingers to count along as she presents a list.	
A student looks at a classmate at the front of the classroom before switching to someone sitting in the back.	

Please note that excerpts and passages in the StudySync® library and this workbook are intended as touchstones to generate interest in an author's work. The excerpts and passages do not substitute for the reading of entire texts, and StudySync® strongly recommends that students seek out and purchase the whole literary or informational work in order to experience it as the author intended. Links to online resellers are available in our digital library. In addition, complete works may be ordered through an authorized reseller by filling out and returning to StudySync® the order form enclosed in this workbook.

Reading & Writing Companion 147

WRITE

Take turns reading your presentation aloud to a partner.

When you are presenting:

- Employ steady eye contact to help keep your listeners' attention.
- Use an appropriate speaking rate, volume, and enunciation to clearly communicate with your listeners.
- Use natural gestures to add meaning and interest as you speak.
- Keep in mind conventions of language, and avoid informal or slang speech.

When you finish, write a reflection about your experience of communicating ideas. How clearly did you speak while giving your presentation? How well did you use eye contact, speaking rate, volume, enunciation, gestures, and conventions of language to communicate your ideas? How can you better communicate your ideas in the future?

REASONS AND
RELEVANT EVIDENCE

Skill: Reasons
and Relevant Evidence

In order to identify if a speaker's argument and specific claims are sound, note the following:

- the argument the speaker is making

- the claim (or claims) that the speaker is making in his or her argument

- the evidence the speaker is using to support this claim

- the logical reasoning the speaker is using

In order to determine the relevancy and sufficiency of the evidence that a speaker is using to support his or her claim(s), use the following questions as a guide:

- Does the speaker use sufficient evidence to support the claim?

- Does the speaker's evidence clearly and logically support the claim?

- Are the speaker's reasoning and evidence sound?

⟳ YOUR TURN

Read the section of Mica's presentation about the article "The Power of Student Peer Leaders" below. Then, complete the chart by identifying the argument and specific claims of the section.

What we read should inspire us and connect directly to our lives. I think that it is important middle school students like us all take the time to read "The Power of Student Peer Leaders." This is a valuable article to read because it will inspire readers with the true story of a fellow student, familiarize them with the college application process, and remind them of the importance of student leadership.

	Argument and Claims
A	This article will inspire readers with the true story of a student and his successful journey.
B	This article will teach readers about the power of student leadership, and how it positively impacts student leaders and other students around them.
C	Everyone should read "The Power of Student Peer Leaders."
D	After reading this, readers will be more familiar with the college application process and better equipped to navigate it in the future.

Argument	
Claim 1	
Claim 2	
Claim 3	

YOUR TURN

Complete the chart below by reading the claim, reasoning, and evidence and then writing in the third column to explain whether the reasoning and evidence are clear and sound. The first one has been completed for you.

Claim	Reasoning and Evidence	Explain
This article will inspire readers with the true story of a student and his successful journey.	Moises was a struggling homeless student in high school. His life changed when he joined a student leadership organization; the organization helped him apply to three colleges and complete the Fasfa. He become a student leader at his school and helped support other students on their journey to college.	The reasoning and evidence are strong because the writer offers many pieces of evidence that clearly and logically support the claim.
After reading this, readers will be more familiar with the college application process and better equipped to navigate it in the future.	The article explains how Moises, who is now a junior in college at the State University of New York at Albany, wrote a personal essay for his college application.	
This article will teach readers about the power of student leadership and how it positively impacts student leaders and other students around them.	After being trained as a peer leader, Moises applied to three colleges and applied for financial aid through Fasfa. He grew his confidence in public speaking. He also worked to create a campaign to increase the college application rate at his school, and it increased to 95% from 69%.	

Please note that excerpts and passages in the StudySync® library and this workbook are intended as touchstones to generate interest in an author's work. The excerpts and passages do not substitute for the reading of entire texts, and StudySync® strongly recommends that students seek out and purchase the whole literary or informational work in order to experience it as the author intended. Links to online resellers are available in our digital library. In addition, complete works may be ordered through an authorized reseller by filling out and returning to StudySync® the order form enclosed in this workbook.

Reading & Writing Companion   **151**

Skill:
Sources and Citations

In your presentation, provide citations for any information that you obtained from an outside source. This includes the following:

- direct quotations
- paraphrased information
- tables, charts, and data
- images
- videos
- audio files

Your citations should be as brief and unobtrusive as possible. Follow these general guidelines:

- The citation should indicate the author's last name and the page number(s) on which the information appears (if the source has numbered pages), enclosed in parentheses.
- If the author is not known, the citation should list the title of the work.

At the end of your presentation, include a slide with your works cited list, following the formatting guidelines of a standard and accepted format. These are the elements and the order in which they should be listed for works cited entries:

- author
- title of source
- publisher
- publication date
- location
- for web sources, the URL

Not all of these elements will apply to each citation, and there are often exceptions. Include only the elements that are relevant for the source. Consult with your teacher as needed.

↻ YOUR TURN

Complete the chart by listing the elements and examples in the correct order according to the standard formatting style for a works cited list.

	Elements and Examples
A	Confessore, Nick
B	publication
C	author
D	23 Jan. 2019
E	"He Reported on Facebook. Now He Approaches It With Caution."
F	https://www.nytimes.com/2019/01/23/technology/personaltech/facebook-online-privacy.html?rref=collection%2Ftimestopic%2FSocial%20Media&action=click&contentCollection=timestopics&region=stream&module=stream_unit&version=latest&contentPlacement=4&pgtype=collection
G	*The New York Times*
H	URL
I	publication date
J	title of source

Element	Example

WRITE

Use the questions in the checklist section to create or revise your citations and works cited list. Make sure that each slide with researched information briefly identifies the source of the information. When you have completed your citations, compile a list of all your sources and write out your works cited list. Refer to an MLA style guide or the style guide required by your teacher as needed.

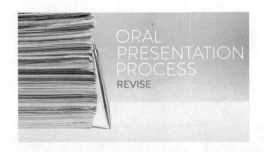

Oral Presentation Process: Revise

| PLAN | DRAFT | REVISE | EDIT AND PRESENT |

You have written a draft of your oral presentation. You have also received input from your peers about how to improve it. Now you are going to revise your draft.

◀◀ REVISION GUIDE

Examine your draft to find areas for revision. Keep in mind your purpose and audience as you revise for clarity, development, organization, and style. Use the guide below to help you review:

Review	Revise	Example
Clarity		
Identify places where more information or details would clarify the points that you present.	Add important information so your readers will understand whom or what you are discussing.	But I think it's worth taking a chance on an episode of *The Twilight Zone* series called "The Monsters Are Due on Maple Street."

Review	Revise	Example
Development		
Identify ideas in your presentation that are not developed with evidence and reasons. Annotate places where your argument lacks support.	Focus on a single claim and add details that help explain your ideas.	Knowing that something bad might happen makes you want to watch every scene closely. The episode's plot is full of surprises that will make your jaw drop and your heart pound in your chest. You never know what is going to happen next.
Organization		
Use transitions when switching between ideas or topics. Annotate places where the topic changes in your oral presentation.	Add short transitions that show the connections between your ideas within and across paragraphs.	Serling created "The Monsters Are Due on Maple Street" in response to a rising distrust between some Americans. The actions of the neighbors on Maple Street can be seen as commentary on the paranoia associated with the Red Scare. However, this episode wasn't just entertainment or a history lesson; it's also a life lesson.
Style: Word Choice		
Identify paragraphs or sentences that repeat the same word.	Replace overly repetitive vocabulary with a synonym.	"The Monsters Are Due on Maple Street" also grabs your attention through its tense and ~~attention-grabbing~~ suspenseful action.

Review	Revise	Example
Style: Sentence Variety		
Look for series of sentences that have similar lengths. Annotate any places where a conjunction or transition could vary the length of sentences you use.	Shorten a section of long sentences or join shorter sentences together.	"The Monsters Are Due on Maple Street" was written in 1960, just years after the Red Scare ~~, which was~~. The Red Scare was a time in American history when many people were fearful of communist politics. During the Red Scare, many people were spying on neighbors to uncover secret communists~~, some~~. Some people were arrested. "Reds" was a nickname for communists at the time. Serling created "The Monsters Are Due on Maple Street" in response to a rising distrust between some Americans.

✏ WRITE

Use the guide above, as well as your peer reviews, to help you evaluate your oral presentation to determine areas that should be revised.

Once you have finished revising your draft, you can then focus on determining how you will deliver your presentation, practicing reading it aloud and noting key words or phrases you want to emphasize. You can also create the visual and multimedia components that will accompany the presentation, making sure they are clear and engaging.

Please note that excerpts and passages in the StudySync® library and this workbook are intended as touchstones to generate interest in an author's work. The excerpts and passages do not substitute for the reading of entire texts, and StudySync® strongly recommends that students seek out and purchase the whole literary or informational work in order to experience it as the author intended. Links to online resellers are available in our digital library. In addition, complete works may be ordered through an authorized reseller by filling out and returning to StudySync® the order form enclosed in this workbook.

Reading & Writing Companion   157

Grammar: Economy of Language

In general, writing should be as brief as possible while still containing all the meaning an author wishes to convey. Any words that do not add to that meaning should be deleted. Writing that contains unnecessary, imprecise, or repetitive words is considered to be wordy. Wordiness is a sign of weak or unedited writing.

A knowledge of economy of language can help an author edit for wordiness. "Economy," in this usage, means "efficient, using the fewest possible words to write a sentence."

Strategy	Edited for Wordiness	Not Yet Edited for Wordiness
Use one or two words to take the place of an awkward or imprecise description.	The **distant** tiger growled loud enough for them to hear.	The tiger, which was very far ahead of them in the distance, growled loud enough for them to hear.
Replace multi-word terms with single-word synonyms.	**Because** food costs are rising, the school board announced that lunch prices will go up **soon**.	Due to the fact that food costs are rising, the school board announced that lunch prices will go up in the not-too-distant future.
Choose specific nouns, verbs, and adjectives instead of awkward or long description.	Omar **assumed** that Sarah **admired** his **leadership** in the study group.	Omar thought, but could not say for sure, that Sarah respected and approved of the way he could guide and direct everyone in the study group.
Eliminate words, phrases, or sentences that repeat information.	Twice a week, Pierre played tennis with Yvette. She was a top player on the school's tennis team.	Twice a week, Pierre played tennis with Yvette. She was a good athlete. She was a member of and top player on the school's tennis team.

YOUR TURN

1. How should this sentence be edited to reduce wordiness?

   > Elena had to drop out of college on account of the fact that her family needed her financial support.

   - A. Replace **had to drop** with **had dropped**.
   - B. Replace **on account of the fact that** with **because**.
   - C. Delete **financial support**.
   - D. No change needs to be made to this sentence.

2. How should this sentence be edited to reduce wordiness?

   > Not all people believe that a college education should cost something; some people believe it should cost nothing. There are many opinions on the subject.

   - A. Delete **There are many opinions on the subject.**
   - B. Delete **; some people believe it should cost nothing**.
   - C. Delete **; some people believe it should cost nothing. There are many opinions on the subject**.
   - D. No change needs to be made to this sentence.

3. How should this sentence be edited to reduce wordiness?

   > Donna took me to a theme park and it was a very fascinating place to be.

   - A. We went to a theme park and had a fascinating time.
   - B. I was taken by Donna to a fascinating theme park.
   - C. Donna took me to a fascinating theme park.
   - D. No change needs to be made to this sentence.

4. How should this sentence be edited to reduce wordiness?

   > Sara Jane often wrote songs for the high school glee club, that being the organization which frequently performed her work, and later wrote the score for a Broadway musical.

   - A. Delete **that being the organization which frequently performed her work**.
   - B. Delete **that being the organization**.
   - C. Delete **that being**.
   - D. No change needs to be made to this sentence.

Grammar:
Noun Clauses

A clause is a group of words that contains both a subject and a verb. A noun clause is a subordinate clause that acts as a noun in a sentence.

A noun clause usually begins with one of these words: *how, that, what, whatever, when, where, which, whichever, who, whom, whoever, whose,* or *why.* To identify most noun clauses, locate a clause with one of these words. Then, replace the noun clause with a pronoun such as *she, he, it,* or *they.* The sentence should still make sense.

Locate Noun Clause	Replace with a Pronoun
Do you remember **when we watched the movie**?	Do you remember **it**?

You can use a noun clause in the same ways you use a noun—as a subject, a direct object, an indirect object, an object of a preposition, and a predicate noun.

Function of Clause	Text
Object of a Preposition	Yet networks do need to take some responsibility for **what they have created with reality TV**. Reality TV and Society
Direct Object	Network executives don't understand **what they have created with reality TV**.
Subject	**What they have created** is having a negative impact on TV and society.
Predicate Noun	Reality TV is **what they have created**.

↻ YOUR TURN

1. Replace the words in bold with a noun clause.

    > **The lady at the front desk** will check out your books.

    ○ A. Either the manager or her assistant
    ○ B. The woman with the name tag
    ○ C. Whoever works at the front desk
    ○ D. No change needs to be made to this sentence.

2. Replace the words in bold with a noun clause.

    > **The person with the most experience** will likely get the job offer.

    ○ A. The most experienced person
    ○ B. Whoever has the most experience
    ○ C. Experiencing the most
    ○ D. No change needs to be made to this sentence.

3. Replace the words in bold with a noun clause.

    > .The teacher talked about **how his students worked very hard yesterday**.

    ○ A. working very hard yesterday
    ○ B. the hardworking students
    ○ C. worked the hardest while in his class
    ○ D. No change needs to be made to this sentence.

4. Replace the words in bold with a noun clause.

    > During lunch, all of the students ate **the cafeteria's pizza**.

    ○ A. what the cafeteria made that day
    ○ B. delicious cafeteria food
    ○ C. eating the pizza
    ○ D. No change needs to be made to this sentence.

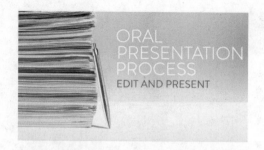

Oral Presentation Process: Edit and Present

| PLAN | DRAFT | REVISE | EDIT AND PRESENT |

You have revised your oral presentation based on your peer feedback and your own examination. Now, it is time to edit your presentation. When you revised, you focused on the content of your presentation. You probably practiced communicating your ideas and considering your audience and purpose. When you edit, you focus on the mechanics of your presentation, paying close attention to things like grammar and punctuation.

Use the checklist below to guide you as you edit:

☐ Have I used noun clauses correctly?

☐ Have I edited for economy of language?

☐ Have I spelled everything correctly?

☐ Did I include transitions to create cohesion and clarify ideas in my presentation?

☐ Have I added digital media or visuals to enhance my presentation?

Notice some edits Theo has made:

- Edited to include a noun clause

- Edited for economy of language by combining related sentences to create one shorter sentence

- Edited for economy of language by removing wordy descriptions and shortening sentences

- Added transition words.

- Added in a note to include more visuals.

[slide with an image of a mysterious object flying across sky] First, a strange object passes over the town, causing electronics to stop working. Then, Les Goodman's car starts on its own and people become suspicious,~~.The neighbors think Goodman~~ thinking he might be part of an alien invasion. Goodman struggles to explain ~~the strange event.~~ what is happening to him. He says, "So I've got a car that starts by itself . . . I don't know why the car works—it just does!" Neither the characters nor the viewers know what to believe. ~~As the people of Maple Street get more worried, you want to pick a side: either Les Goodman is innocent or it he is hiding dangerous secrets. However, there are no clear answers in "The Monsters Are Due on Maple Street." Having to decide for yourself makes watching the episode a thrilling experience.~~ Is it aliens? Is it something else? Nobody knows.

✏ WRITE

Use the questions on the previous page, as well as your peer reviews, to help you evaluate your oral presentation to determine areas that need editing. Then edit your presentation to correct those errors. Finally, rehearse your presentation, including both the delivery of your written work and the strategic use of digital media you plan to incorporate.

Once you have made all your corrections and rehearsed with your digital media selections, you are ready to present your work. You may present to your class or to a group of peers. You can record your presentation to share with family and friends or to post on your blog. If you publish online, share the link with your family, friends, and classmates.

The Monsters Backstage

DRAMA

Introduction

"The Monsters Backstage" is set in the moments before the curtain rises on a high school play. After the lead actor's wig mysteriously goes missing, the characters try to figure out what happened. Tensions rise as the actors' focus turns from the play to their suspicions of each other. Will they find the wig? Is one of the actors responsible for its disappearance? Whether or not they find answers to these questions, the show must go on.

V VOCABULARY

rehearse
to practice a performance

sabotage
to destroy something on purpose

mannequin
a figure that is shaped like a human body and is used for making or displaying clothes

accusation
a statement that claims someone has done something wrong

ridiculous
absurd or unreasonable

≡ READ

NOTES

1 [SCENE: *It is the opening night of a high school play.* EMMA, OLIVIA, TYLER, *and* CHRIS *wear costumes inspired by clothing from the late 1800s. The curtain is down. The actors hear the audience members talking.* EMMA *and* CHRIS *exchange worried glances.* TYLER *plays on his phone. As the scene opens,* OLIVIA *applies lipstick.*]

2 OLIVIA [*smiling in a mirror*]: Oh, that's perfect! [*She puts the makeup away and faces her castmates.*] Can you believe that it is nearly showtime? The time spent **rehearsing** is about to pay off. The curtain will rise soon, so break a leg! I'm confident this play will be a smash!

3 CHRIS: Of course you are. You've starred in plays since second grade. Emma and I are terrified!

4 OLIVIA: You'll be great! Tyler, I recommend that you put down the phone. I need one finishing touch. Emma, can you get my wig? I put it on the **mannequin** after dress rehearsal.

5   EMMA [*walks offstage and returns empty-handed*]: There is nothing on the mannequin's head. Are you sure that's where you left your wig?

6   OLIVIA [*annoyed*]: Yes.

7   EMMA: That's weird. It's not as if we have monsters backstage who take our stuff. Maybe someone accidentally moved it.

8   OLIVIA [*panicking*]: Help me find it!

9   [CHRIS *and* EMMA *walk off stage, whispering to each other.*]

10   TYLER [*rolling his eyes*]: Do you even need the wig?

11   OLIVIA: Don't be **ridiculous**. The wig helps me get into character. I bet you hid it. Is that your idea of a joke, or did you want to **sabotage** the play? You clearly do not want to be here!

12   TYLER [*suddenly angry*]: Now who's being ridiculous? I skipped basketball practice to rehearse for this play! I bet the Stage Fright Twins hid your wig so we can't go on.

13   [CHRIS *and* EMMA *enter, shaking their heads.*]

14   OLIVIA: Did you hide my wig to stop the play? I can't believe it.

15   EMMA [*shocked*]: That's because you shouldn't. If I hid your wig, why was I just looking for it? Use your brain! These wild **accusations** cause trouble. We should work together to find a solution.

16   OLIVIA: Like how you and Chris worked together to find a solution for your stage fright?

17   CHRIS: Or maybe Olivia hid her own wig to get more attention. Is that it?

18   [EMMA, OLIVIA, TYLER, *and* CHRIS *shout at each other. Suddenly, the curtain rises. The actors see the audience and freeze.*]

First Read

Read the play. After you read, answer the Think Questions below.

☁ THINK QUESTIONS

1. Who are the characters in the play? What are they doing?

   _____

   _____

2. Write two or three sentences describing the problems that the characters face.

   _____

   _____

3. Which characters are nervous about the play, and how do you know?

   _____

   _____

4. Use context to confirm the meaning of the word *sabotage* as it is used in "The Monsters Backstage." Write your definition of *sabotage* here.

   _____

   _____

5. What is another way to say that an idea is *ridiculous*?

   _____

   _____

Skill:
Analyzing Expressions

★ DEFINE

When you read, you may find English expressions that you do not know. An **expression** is a group of words that communicates an idea. Three types of expressions are idioms, sayings, and figurative language. They can be difficult to understand because the meanings of the words are different from their **literal**, or usual, meanings.

An **idiom** is an expression that is commonly known among a group of people. For example, "It's raining cats and dogs" means it is raining heavily. **Sayings** are short expressions that contain advice or wisdom. For instance, "Don't count your chickens before they hatch" means do not plan on something good happening before it happens. **Figurative** language is when you describe something by comparing it with something else, either directly (using the words *like* or *as*) or indirectly. For example, "I'm as hungry as a horse" means I'm very hungry. None of the expressions are about actual animals.

••• CHECKLIST FOR ANALYZING EXPRESSIONS

To determine the meaning of an expression, remember the following:

✓ If you find a confusing group of words, it may be an expression. The meaning of words in expressions may not be their literal meaning.

- Ask yourself: Is this confusing because the words are new? Or because the words do not make sense together?

✓ Determining the overall meaning may require that you use one or more of the following:

- context clues

- a dictionary or other resource

- teacher or peer support

✓ Highlight important information before and after the expression to look for clues.

YOUR TURN

Read the excerpts and the literal meaning of each expression. Write the expression's meaning as it is used in the text into the correct row.

	Meaning in the Text
A	think
B	good luck with a theatrical performance
C	start the performance

#	Excerpt	Literal Meaning	Meaning in the Text
1	OLIVIA [*smiling in a mirror*]: ... The time spent rehearsing is about to pay off. The curtain will rise soon, so **break a leg**! I'm confident this play will be a smash!	break a bone in the leg	
2	EMMA [*shocked*]: That's because you shouldn't. If I hid your wig, why was I just looking for it? **Use your brain**! These wild accusations cause trouble. We should work together to find a solution.	use the organ in your head that controls your body's activities	
3	TYLER [*suddenly angry*]: ... I bet the Stage Fright Twins hid your wig so we can't **go on**.	continue	

Skill:
Analyzing and Evaluating Text

★ DEFINE

Analyzing and **evaluating** a text means reading carefully to understand the author's **purpose** and **message**. In informational texts, authors may provide information or opinions on a topic. They may be writing to inform or persuade a reader. In fictional texts, the author may be **communicating** a message or lesson through their story. They may write to entertain, or to teach the reader something about life.

Sometimes authors are clear about their message and purpose. When the message or purpose is not stated directly, readers will need to look closer at the text. Readers can use text evidence to make inferences about what the author is trying to communicate. By analyzing and evaluating the text, you can form your own thoughts and opinions about what you read.

••• CHECKLIST FOR ANALYZING AND EVALUATING TEXT

In order to analyze and evaluate a text, do the following:

✓ Look for details that show *why* the author is writing.

- Ask yourself: Is the author trying to inform, persuade, or entertain? What are the main ideas of this text?

✓ Look for details that show *what* the author is trying to say.

- Ask yourself: What is the author's opinion about this topic? Is there a lesson I can learn from this story?

✓ Form your own thoughts and opinions about the text.

- Ask yourself: Do I agree with the author? Does this message apply to my life?

YOUR TURN

Read the following excerpt from the story. Then, complete the multiple-choice questions below.

---

from "The Monsters Backstage"

9   [CHRIS *and* EMMA *walk off stage, whispering to each other.*]

10   TYLER [*rolling his eyes*]: Do you even need the wig?

11   OLIVIA: Don't be ridiculous. The wig helps me get into character. I bet you hid it. Is that your idea of a joke, or did you want to sabotage the play? You clearly do not want to be here!

12   TYLER [*suddenly angry*]: Now who's being ridiculous? I skipped basketball practice to rehearse for this play! I bet the Stage Fright Twins hid your wig so we can't go on.

---

1. What is the author trying to show in the excerpt?

   ○ A. Tyler hid Olivia's wig so that he could spend more time on his phone.
   ○ B. Two other characters hid Olivia's wig to ruin the play.
   ○ C. Olivia cannot do the play without her wig, and so she is ready to quit.
   ○ D. Despite what Olivia thinks, Tyler wants the play to go on.

2. What text evidence helped you infer this?

   ○ A. Emma and Chris are whispering to each other.
   ○ B. Tyler asks Olivia if she even needs the wig.
   ○ C. Olivia thinks Tyler hid the wig as a joke.
   ○ D. Tyler skipped basketball practice to rehearse the play.

THE MONSTERS
BACKSTAGE

Close Read

 WRITE

NARRATIVE: In this play, a missing wig causes distrust and conflict backstage. Select a character, and describe the events of the story from his or her point of view. How does your character feel? What does he or she think? What message or lesson does he or she learn? Pay attention to irregularly spelled words as you write.

Use the checklist below to guide you as you write.

☐ What does your character do during the play?

☐ What emotions does your character experience during the play?

☐ What does your character think about the other characters and the situation?

☐ What lesson does your character learn?

Use the sentence frames to organize and write your narrative.

My name is _____. Before the play, I _____, and I was _____.

The others needed to _____, so I _____.

Then I _____, but _____.

I was _____. I even _____.

We all started to _____.

I learned a valuable lesson. I learned that it is important to _____.

 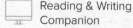

Peer Pressure vs. Teenagers

ARGUMENTATIVE TEXT

Introduction

Peer pressure is something everyone has to deal with, but it especially affects teenagers. In this text, learn what peer pressure is and what researchers have discovered about this phenomenon that has such a strong hold over the lives

V VOCABULARY

influence

to affect people

cognitive

involving brain activity

psychologist

a person who studies behavior and the mind

achieve

to reach a goal

risky

having a danger of loss or injury

NOTES

≡ READ

1   Nearly everyone has experienced peer pressure. A peer is someone who is the same age as you. Peer pressure is **influence** from peers. People, especially teenagers, behave differently when they experience peer pressure.

2   Peer pressure may cause young people to make bad choices. When teenagers behave badly, is it because they are trying to make their friends think they're cool? Researchers have been attempting to answer this question.

3   **Psychologists** have studied the effects of peer pressure on adolescents. Brett Laursen is a professor of psychology at Florida Atlantic University. Laursen says peer pressure "begins as soon as children start to pay attention to what other children think about them." Peer pressure will become even stronger as young people gain more control over their daily lives. Kevin M. King is a psychology professor at the University of Washington. King explains that students in middle school and high school have increasing freedom to

make choices. As children get older and more aware of other people's opinions, the effects of peer pressure can become more serious.

4   Peer pressure can affect students. In Sweden, researchers studied children who have friends that feel exhausted from school. These children often showed less interest in school themselves. Another study had adolescents play a driving computer game. Then the researchers told the players that they were being watched by peers in another room. The players' driving became more **risky**. The players crashed more frequently. Peer pressure can make driving and other activities more risky. Teenagers may get hurt or make bad decisions.

5   Researchers Dustin Albert, Jason Chein, and Laurence Steinberg have found that the structure of the brain may be why peer pressure affects teenagers more than other age groups. When younger teenagers do something risky and their friends like it, the brain records this "reward." The teenager becomes more likely to repeat the behavior. This makes it more likely something bad will happen to the teenager. As a teenager grows older, the brain's **cognitive** control system matures. Then it is easier for the teen to resist peer pressure.

6   How should teenagers deal with peer pressure? The answer is to make it work to their advantage. Laursen points out that children can do better academically when they study with friends who **achieve** at a higher level. These friends can give a push, in a friendly way, to get the person to work harder.

First Read

Read the text. After you read, answer the Think Questions below.

☁ **THINK QUESTIONS**

1. What is peer pressure?

_____

_____

2. What are the dangers of peer pressure?

_____

_____

3. Write two or three sentences describing how a teenager who is not doing well in school can deal with peer pressure.

_____

_____

4. Use context to confirm the meaning of the word *psychologist* as it is used in "Peer Pressure vs. Teenagers." Write your definition of *psychologist* here.

_____

_____

5. What is another way to say that an action is *risky*?

_____

_____

Skill:
Language Structures

★ DEFINE

In every language, there are rules that tell how to **structure** sentences. These rules define the correct order of words. In the English language, for example, a **basic** structure for sentences is subject, verb, and object. Some sentences have more **complicated** structures.

You will encounter both basic and complicated **language structures** in the classroom materials you read. Being familiar with language structures will help you better understand the text.

••• CHECKLIST FOR LANGUAGE STRUCTURES

To improve your comprehension of language structures, do the following:

 Monitor your understanding.

- Ask yourself: Why do I not understand this sentence? Is it because I do not understand some of the words? Or is it because I do not understand the way the words are ordered in the sentence?

✓ Pay attention to **perfect tenses** as you read. There are three perfect tenses in the English language: the present perfect, past perfect, and future perfect.

- **Present perfect tense** can be used to indicate a situation that began at a prior point in time and continues into the present.
  - > Combine *have* or *has* with the past participle of the main verb.
    Example: I **have played** basketball for three years.

- **Past perfect tense** can describe an action that happened before another action or event in the past.
  - > Combine *had* with the past participle of the main verb.
    Example: I **had learned** how to dribble a ball before I could walk!

- **Future perfect tense** expresses one future action that will begin and end before another future event begins or before a certain time.
  - > Use *will have* or *shall have* with the past participle of a verb.
    Example: Before the end of the year, I **will have played** more than 100 games!

✓ Break down the sentence into its parts.

- Ask yourself: What actions are expressed in this sentence? Are they completed or are they ongoing? What words give me clues about when an action is taking place?

✓ Confirm your understanding with a peer or teacher.

YOUR TURN

Notice the perfect tense in each sentence. Write each sentence into the correct column.

Sentences	
A	Before next week, we will have finished this chapter.
B	I walked home after the game had ended.
C	I have finished my homework.
D	The tickets will have sold out by this evening.
E	She has won.
F	I had finished my homework before you called.

Present Perfect	Past Perfect	Future Perfect

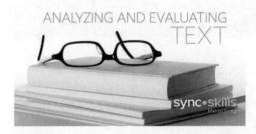

Skill:
Analyzing and Evaluating Text

★ DEFINE

Analyzing and **evaluating** a text means reading carefully to understand the author's **purpose** and **message**. In informational texts, authors may provide information or opinions on a topic. They may be writing to inform or persuade a reader. In fictional texts, the author may be **communicating** a message or lesson through their story. They may write to entertain, or to teach the reader something about life.

Sometimes authors are clear about their message and purpose. When the message or purpose is not stated directly, readers will need to look closer at the text. Readers can use text evidence to make inferences about what the author is trying to communicate. By analyzing and evaluating the text, you can form your own thoughts and opinions about what you read.

••• CHECKLIST FOR ANALYZING AND EVALUATING TEXT

In order to analyze and evaluate a text, do the following:

✓ Look for details that show *why* the author is writing.

   • Ask yourself: Is the author trying to inform, persuade, or entertain? What are the main ideas of this text?

✓ Look for details that show *what* the author is trying to say.

   • Ask yourself: What is the author's opinion about this topic? Is there a lesson I can learn from this story?

✓ Form your own thoughts and opinions about the text.

   • Ask yourself: Do I agree with the author? Does this message apply to my life?

Please note that excerpts and passages in the StudySync® library and this workbook are intended as touchstones to generate interest in an author's work. The excerpts and passages do not substitute for the reading of entire texts, and StudySync® strongly recommends that students seek out and purchase the whole literary or informational work in order to experience it as the author intended. Links to online resellers are available in our digital library. In addition, complete works may be ordered through an authorized reseller by filling out and returning to StudySync® the order form enclosed in this workbook.

YOUR TURN

Read the following excerpt from the text. Then, complete the multiple-choice questions below.

---

from "Peer Pressure vs. Teenagers"

Researchers Dustin Albert, Jason Chein, and Laurence Steinberg have found that the structure of the brain may be why peer pressure affects teenagers more than other age groups. When younger teenagers do something risky and their friends like it, the brain records this "reward." The teenager becomes more likely to repeat the behavior. This makes it more likely something bad will happen to the teenager. As a teenager grows older, the brain's cognitive control system matures. Then it is easier for the teen to resist peer pressure.

---

1. What is the author's purpose for this text?

   ○ A. to persuade
   ○ B. to entertain
   ○ C. to inform
   ○ D. to provide an opinion

2. What message is the author trying to communicate in this paragraph?

   ○ A. Teenagers need activities to help their brains develop.
   ○ B. Teenagers like to repeat the same behaviors.
   ○ C. As teenagers age, their brains mature.
   ○ D. As teenagers grow older, the structure of their brains mature, and they are able to more easily resist peer pressure.

PEER PRESSURE
VS. TEENAGERS

Close Read

✏ WRITE

ARGUMENTATIVE: At the end of the article, the author suggests that peer pressure can be useful for teens. How can it be useful? Do you agree or disagree? Write a short paragraph that analyzes and evaluates the author's position. Include your own position and ideas, and use details from the text to support your claim. Pay attention to main verbs and helping verbs as you write.

Use the checklist below to guide you as you write.

☐ How does the author say that peer pressure can be useful?

☐ Why do you agree or disagree with the author?

☐ What text details support your opinion?

Use the sentence frames to organize and write your argument.

The author suggests that peer pressure can be useful for teens when _____.

I think the author is _____.

The author's _____ is a _____ idea.

If a student is _____, it can definitely _____.

But _____.

Peer pressure can be _____ for teens.

Please note that excerpts and passages in the StudySync® library and this workbook are intended as touchstones to generate interest in an author's work. The excerpts and passages do not substitute for the reading of entire texts, and StudySync® strongly recommends that students seek out and purchase the whole literary or informational work in order to experience it as the author intended. Links to online resellers are available in our digital library. In addition, complete works may be ordered through an authorized reseller by filling out and returning to StudySync® the order form enclosed in this workbook.

Reading & Writing
Companion

181

PHOTO/IMAGE CREDITS:

studysync®

Text Fulfillment Through StudySync

If you are interested in specific titles, please fill out the form below and we will check availability through our partners.

ORDER DETAILS

Date:

TITLE	AUTHOR	Paperback/ Hardcover	Specific Edition *If Applicable*	Quantity

SHIPPING INFORMATION

Contact:

Title:

School/District:

Address Line 1:

Address Line 2:

Zip or Postal Code:

Phone:

Mobile:

Email:

BILLING INFORMATION ☐ SAME AS SHIPPING

Contact:

Title:

School/District:

Address Line 1:

Address Line 2:

Zip or Postal Code:

Phone:

Mobile:

Email:

PAYMENT INFORMATION

☐ CREDIT CARD

Name on Card:

Card Number: Expiration Date: Security Code:

☐ PO

Purchase Order Number:

StudySync Text Fulfillment, BookheadEd Learning, LLC
610 Daniel Young Drive | Sonoma, CA 95476